Undiscovered Islands of the Mediterranean

Undiscovered Islands of the Mediterranean

Linda Lancione Moyer
and
Burl Willes

John Muir Publications
Santa Fe, New Mexico

An RDR Syndicate Book
John Muir Publications, P.O. Box 613, Santa Fe, NM 87504

First edition. First printing

Library of Congress Cataloging-in-Publication Data
Moyer, Linda Lancione.
    Undiscovered islands of the Mediterranean / Linda Lancione
Moyer and Burl Willes. — 1st ed.
       p.   cm.
    ISBN 0-945465-53-X
    1. Mediterranean Region—Description and travel—1981- —
Guide-books. 2. Islands—Mediterranean Sea—Guide-books. I.
Willes, Burl, 1941-   . II. Title.
D973.M77   1990
· 910'.91822—dc20   90-7125
                                                            CIP

Distributed to the book trade by:
W.W. Norton & Company, Inc.
New York, New York

Illustrations: V.L. Costa
Cover art: Holly Wood
Maps: Holly Wood
Photos: Linda Lancione Moyer
Typography: Copygraphics, Inc.
Printer: McNaughton & Gunn, Inc.

CONTENTS

CONTENTS

ACKNOWLEDGMENTS

Where shall we go next? What is it like? Will you come with us? How shall we tell about it? Getting answers to these questions from friends and strangers was one of the great pleasures of writing this book. Tanya Gregory Cipolla gave us an insider's view of Italy with her research and affectionate insights on Procida. Miryana Popovich of the Yugoslav National Tourist Office, Bill Zacha, Margaret Titus, and Adam Eterovich helped guide us through Yugoslavia. Sandy McCulloch discovered the island of Milos and wrote about it for us and contributed his splendid photographs and his joyous enthusiasm for Greece. Thanks to fellow travelers Françoise Moreau and Elaine Eisenstadt. We are grateful to Roger Rapoport, Peter Beren, Meredith Bruce, and Jane Phillips for their behind-the-scenes help. Thank-you also to the excellent staff at JMP.

INTRODUCTION

A *re* there any undiscovered islands in the Mediterranean? This was often the response when we told people about our plans to write this book. We were a bit skeptical ourselves. Maybe the lesser-known islands are undiscovered with good reason, we thought. But after sunning in a funky nudist colony, climbing an active volcano, swimming in a grotto more splendid than Capri, strolling in a fragrant pine forest, lounging on a Venetian balcony, wandering through blinding white Cycladic villages, and communing with goats among the ruins of a medieval castle, we now wonder how we could have doubted.

Need we sing the praises of geography? The climate is mild year-round in the Mediterranean region. Hot days are often tempered by the regional wind, familiarly named *mistral* in France, *scirocco* in Italy, *bora* in Yugoslavia, *meltemi* in Greece. We ran out of adjectives to describe the glorious colors of the water, consistently pure and inviting. Most of the islands, low on water and long denuded of forest, are covered with maquis, the low, herb-scented scrub subtle in its beauty against a background of colored earth and stone.

The islands have their charm at any time of year. We had the good fortune to travel in spring and fall, when the weather was ideal and the facilities for visitors virtually empty. Are you willing to risk a storm or two and really isolate yourself in a lovely place? Vito Russo, native of Stromboli and owner of La Sirenetta, a local hotel, loves to return home in the winter from his travels as a mechanical engineer. "The weather is often beautiful, there is no one in the streets at 7:00 in the morning, and by 4:00 in the afternoon it is dark." We feel safe in saying you can travel almost anywhere without hotel reservations, except in July and August or during special holidays.

Just how undiscovered *are* these islands? We cannot say we were ever the *only* tourists in a place, but we came close a couple of times in Yugoslavia and Greece during September and October. We *can* say we were frequently the only North Americans. Tourists are usually from Great Britain and northern Europe, or they are natives of the country in search of a quiet holiday by the sea.

The inevitable question is, won't we spoil these places by telling about them? We don't think so. Many of the islands were once so poor that a large proportion of their inhabitants emigrated to large cities or to Australia and North America. Vacationers infuse life and money into islands that are now underpopulated. In addition, many islands are protected from unbridled growth by strict limits on construction; others have no investment capital to develop a tourist infrastructure. Water shortages also place constraints on the possible number of visitors.

Of course, whether a place is "spoiled" or not depends not only on the number of tourists but also on what kind of visitors they are and what they expect. Accepting a place as it is can mean forgoing high standards of plumbing or strict schedules. You will be rewarded with rich beauty and unparalleled hospitality. "How do you feel about tourists?" we asked a restaurant owner on Kastellorizo. "We don't mind," she smiled, "as long as they're good tourists." So go, enjoy, be a good tourist.

vinc '89

BLACK

SEA

YUGOSLAVIA

Zlarin
Šolta
Vis
Korčula
Biševo
Mljet
Lastovo

Bozcaada
Alibey
TURKEY

Naples

GREECE

CYCLADES

DODECANESE

MALTA

CRETE

AFRICA

5

FRANCE

Îles d'Hyères

Where can you travel an hour by plane from Paris to take long solitary walks, lie on beautiful beaches in warm, breeze-softened sunlight, and eat reasonably priced meals in charming hotels? "*Pas possible,*" you say. No such place. *Mais si.* Go to the Îles d'Hyères, three small islands off the Côte d'Azur, a short boat hop from the old seaside resort of Hyères and the port city of Toulon. These three small nuggets—Porquerolles, Port-Cros, and Île du Levant —are also known with good reason as the Îles d'Or (the Gold Islands). They are all burnished by almost year-round sunshine, frequently polished to cool in the afternoon by the steady mistral. Because Porquerolles and Port-Cros have national park status, growth is severely restricted and flora and fauna are protected. Levant has a very special character and exists within a very limited geographic space, so it is not threatened by growth either. In addition to these assurances of peace and beauty, none of the islands allows cars.

Porquerolles

Porquerolles is a protected island that has been owned by the French government since 1971. The largest and farthest west of the Îles d'Hyères, it is 7.5 kilometers long and 2 kilometers wide. No camping or cars are allowed, nor is any new construction. Busy during the summer with visitors who cross over for a day or vacation in the hotels, it is quiet but not deserted in the spring and fall. Although the hotels and restaurants are full enough to create a friendly ambience, you will probably have no trouble finding a room except during July and August, when reservations should be made well in advance.

The island has an open, expansive feeling as you approach the harbor with its rows of pleasure boats and glimpse the splendid terra-cotta houses strung along the shore. At the harbor there is a tiny information booth, sometimes open when the boat comes in, that gives out brochures about local hotels and sells a little book about the island. Don't expect to get information about other islands here, though; each of the islands in the chain is, or pretends to be, surprisingly ignorant of the others.

Walk up from the long dock to the large dusty square, the Place d'Armes, in the island's only village. An empty, open space, it is surrounded by brightly decorated terrace restaurants and souvenir shops and dominated at the top of its gentle slope by a simple, attractive church.

The village of Porquerolles is on the north coast, which is lined with fine beaches. The south side of the island is mountainous, with cliffs and some stunning views. There are long, well-tended trails for walking or bicycling. Bicycles can be rented in the village for reasonable rates. Some

9

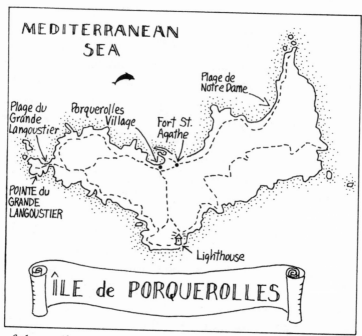

of the trails are quite rocky, so it is best to rent one with puncture-proof tires (*pneus increvables*). Like to sail? Sail-boats can be rented at the harbor for 500-700F ($83-$116) a day or 2,500F ($416) per week, or you can bring your own and dock it in the harbor or anchor it offshore. Motor-boats can be rented for a reasonable rate; prices go up if you do not have a boating license.

This is a place where there is little to do but be at peace with the natural world. Bob Ghiglion, owner of the Relais de la Poste, told us that Clint Eastwood and other movie stars have been known to vacation here (anonymously, of course), taking refuge from the hectic life of Hollywood and the crowded cities of the Côte d'Azur. Don't spend your time looking for celebrities; walk or bicycle down the dry, well-tended paths, lie on the beaches and gaze at the handsome white gulls and black crows flying overhead, watch families at play on the beach or on boats anchored offshore. Let the sunlight, breezes, quiet, and bright colors work on the senses. Have a late afternoon drink while you watch young men and old play *boules* on the square. Take a walk on the jetty after dinner, looking back at the harbor lights. Sleep well.

WALKS

Fort St. Agathe (15 minutes)
Go up the hill behind the village to the old fort for a beautiful view of the island's red-tile rooftops and vegetation and a look down on the port. The pretty apartment build-

ings with balconies and flowers which you pass on your left is, believe it or not, government-subsidized housing.

Lighthouse (1 to 1½ hours)

Go across the island up the hill to the lighthouse. This is a lovely, tree-shaded road with fig, olive, and almond trees growing on either side. Along the way, you will see some ponds where they are experimenting with cleaning the water with algae and insects before recycling it for irrigation.

Plage du Langoustier (2½ to 3 hours)

Go west from the village to the beach at the end of the island, the Plage du Grand Langoustier, part of a small peninsula that has an old fort on it. Here you can look across to the rocky Île du Petit Langoustier. This beach is near the Mas du Langoustier, an extremely secluded upscale hotel that has a glassed-in restaurant overlooking the ocean.

Plage de Notre-Dame (2 hours)

This is a shorter, shadier walk (eastward) to a prettier beach, a gentle curve of fine white sand. Off-season, these beaches are almost empty, although occasionally people from sailboats anchored nearby will come ashore in their Zodiacs (motorized rubber rafts) to sunbathe and swim.

HOW TO GET THERE

This island, closest to the mainland, is most easily reached by taking the small, battered-looking ferry from the tip of the Giens Peninsula, about 15 minutes by taxi from the

Hyères/Toulon airport. This spot is also known as "La Tour Fondue" because of its crumbling old tower. From here, boats leave regularly several times a day, every half hour during July and August, less often during the slower times of the year.

WHERE TO STAY

In addition to the isolated (it has a shuttle bus to take you back and forth to the village and harbor) and exclusive Mas du Langoustier (83540 Île de Porquerolles, Var, France; tel. 94.58.30.09), there are several hotels on Porquerolles, all located on the Place d'Armes. Most require at least a half-board (demi-pension) plan; that is, you must eat either lunch or dinner there.

Hotel des Glycines (83400 Île de Porquerolles, Var, France; tel. 94.58.30.36) has ten rooms and a pretty garden restaurant with a flagstone terrace and stunning color from geraniums and marigolds. Full pension required.

Hotel St. Anne (83400 Île de Porquerolles; tel. 94.58. 30.04) is very pleasant and has friendly management, a pretty dining room, and an outdoor terrace overlooking the square.

Hotel du Relais de la Poste (83540 Île de Porquerolles; tel. 94.58.30.26) is the only hotel on the island that does not have a complete restaurant, leaving you free to pick and choose where to have dinner according to whim. They do serve breakfast and light meals. The proprietors, Bob Ghiglion and his wife, are extremely friendly; his family, of Italian ancestry, has lived on the island for generations. Madame Ghiglion speaks a little English.

Really low-budget accommodations are nonexistent here. Camping is prohibited because of fire hazard. Don't say that you read it here, but we think it would be possible to toss your sleeping bag under a pine tree along the coast without anyone taking too much notice, so long as you don't try to build a fire or put up a tent. In May, at least, we didn't see anyone looking very official.

WHERE TO EAT

Most of the restaurants on the square are in roughly the same price range, so wander around and peruse the menus, choosing what appeals to you. French restaurants are required by law to post their menus and prices. If you order the set-price (prix fixe) "menu," you will get three or four courses that are the selection of the day (sometimes there are two or three options for each course). This is the cheapest and easiest way to order. Ask for "le menu" if you want to eat this way; if you want what we Americans call the menu (the list of foods), ask for "la carte." Some places have two or three set-price menus, starting at about 80F ($13).

Down toward the port, you can get take-away pizzas and sandwiches and mixed salads. Mornings, there is a small street market in the square where you can buy fruit for a picnic. Tucked away between the restaurants are a couple of little grocery stores, but they close at noon or 1:00 p.m. for most of the afternoon. On the road that heads west out of the village toward the beach, there is a dusty little outdoor restaurant called L'Air du Temps, a place to stop for lunch or a drink. On your outings to the beach, be sure to take water or fruit; there is no fresh water available except in the village.

The food in the islands is a representative selection of southern French cooking. Fresh fish is the best bet. The famous bouillabaisse is available but often must be ordered in advance. Other fish soups are also gratifying. They are often served with *la rouille* (literally, rust), mayonnaise blended with red pepper, to be stirred into the soup or spread on toasted bread. You will see plenty of rice and garlic.

Compared with the rest of France, the food in these islands is not outstanding. One can speculate that the distance from land forces a reliance on frozen foods or that standards are lower because these places have captive customers. In this country of gastronomes, I never thought that I would find in the center of my croissant a tiny little frozen core.

You can get wine made on the island by ordering rose or red *du domaine de l'île*.

Port-Cros

Local lore has it that at one time, there were plans afoot to make this one-square-mile island into a hideaway for millionaires, with fancy hotels and helicopter access. Fortunately, in 1961, it was willed to the state as a national park. There are still a few privately owned homes, but no further construction is permitted.

The little town is simply a row of restaurants and shops tightly tucked around the bay and harbor, the maquis-covered mountains rising close and dark behind it. Only a little farther offshore than Porquerolles, Port-Cros feels like a faraway outpost, less a vacation spot than a refuge. Since lodging is extremely limited, it is mostly frequented by day-trippers who come for Sunday lunch or a *promenade* and boaters who tied up in the harbor and come ashore for meals, leaving the splendid long trails virtually empty for those who do come and stay.

In summer, many pleasure boats dock here. The restaurants are full of Germans, English, and Italians, and it can be amusing to watch the waitress struggle with her customers to get the orders straight. Off-season, the day hikers stay home, and there are few boats in the harbor.

There is a park information office at the port (closed

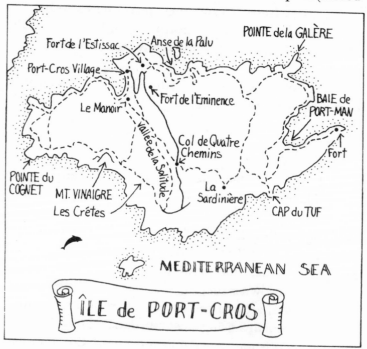

POINTE de la GALÈRE

Fort de l'Estissac — Anse de la Palu

Port-Cros Village —

Fort de l'Eminence

Le Manoir

BAIE de PORT-MAN

Vallée de la Solitude

Col de Quatre Chemins

Fort

POINTE du COGNET   MT. VINAIGRE
Les Crétes

La Sardinière

CAP du TUF

MEDITERRANEAN SEA

ÎLE de PORT-CROS

from noon to midafternoon), but the true information office is at one of the two souvenir shops, the one without a name. Its owner, the blond, affable Bernard, is glad to show you maps of the island and tell you which are the best trails to take. He sells snorkeling equipment and an attractive line of green and white painted pottery. (He also rents snorkeling equipment, but you have to ask for it. It's not on display.)

Porquerolles is informal and unpretentious but still feels like kind of an "in" place. In contrast, people who come to Port-Cros couldn't care less about being trendy. Once, in the harbor, we saw an elderly couple on a pontooned rubber raft rigged up with an orange canvas roof and canvas flaps that let down at night so they could sleep on board. A day-glo sampan.

This is a place to *hike*. One day, we passed two hardy, smiling women of "a certain age," as the French say, using ski poles as walking sticks. You would have thought they were in the Alps. In late May, we walked for miles in splendid weather without seeing "even a cat," to quote our friend Françoise.

WALKS

Here are two good walks. The first takes two leisurely hours; leave a good half day for the second.

Walk #1
From the village, go west and climb up through Le Vallée de la Solitude (Solitude Valley) to Les Crêtes and Mont Vinaigre (Vinegar Mountain). The trail is broad and well tended and overarched by oak trees. Although Port-Cros is known as

the Green Island (l'île Verte), vegetation is far from lush, as it rains very little here. In sunlight, the silvery blue and green of the scarab beetles along the path is the same color as the fabulous sea. Follow the signs to the Pointe du Cognet, where there is a beautiful view of an old fort. It is so quiet here that the splendid huge gulls you are likely to disturb will tell you in no uncertain terms that you are intruding on their terrain. A little farther along, there are some fabulous gull's-eye shots down the cliffs to the swirling inlets below. Then the path drops down gently to the tiny "south beach" and back along the coast to the village, passing by the lovely hotel called Le Manoir. Just outside the village, there is a handsome old chapel constructed from the local rose-colored stone. The rear of the chapel serves as a schoolroom for the handful of children who live on the island year-round.

Walk #2
Another good hike takes off from the village toward the east. Walk up to the little Fort de l'Estissac. This side of the island is a bit less dry than the other and has a few more flowers. There are great views of rock formations and the sea. The mica-rich shale gives everything a silvery cast. Peek into the little walled cemetery nearby with its plastic flowers, rusty wrought-iron crosses, and photos of the departed. Follow the *sentier botanique* (botanical trail), a path of steep stone steps that leads down to the sea. Soon you will come upon the little bay and beach called Anse de la Palu where many boats cast anchor. Unfortunately, their owners also cast their plastic garbage into the sea, which makes for less than appetizing swimming. It is better to

cross the beach and climb up the hill again, walking all the way out to the Pointe de la Galère (or as far as you can go; there is some sort of military presence at the end of the road). Now curve around the end of the island to the south side. The trail skirts the bay of Port-Man, and you can see out to its point and the fort. You are headed toward what is called on the map the Cap du Tuf, but on the trail it is simply marked by a little sign, Tuf. Here, if you are sure-footed,

head down the cliff to the water's edge and spend an hour or an afternoon sitting on the end of the world, surrounded by yellow flowers and fat bumblebees. The easiest way back to the village is inland via la Sardinière and the Col des Quatre Chemins, where you can pick up the island's one paved road and head down to the village again. Shortly before you reach it, you will pass the enormous Fort de l'Eminence, where groups of children attending sailing school are occasionally lodged.

HOW TO GET THERE

In summer (July and August), getting there is easy. Boats travel from Hyères and Le Lavandou between the islands several times a day. In spring and fall, there are boats from Hyères to Port-Cros and other boats that make the Hyères–Port-Cros–Levant–Hyères circuit. In the winter, there *are* boats three or four times a week, but the timetables are not published. Even the regularly scheduled boats are a bit unreliable during the week when there aren't a lot of tourists.

Once, on the dock at Port-Cros, we waited politely with our suitcases while the captain and his assistant unloaded beautiful boxes of peaches and strawberries for the hotel, plus five or ten mattresses. When his cargo was barely off the boat, he untied and chugged off without us. No harm done; he came back later the same afternoon, unscheduled, so we got where we wanted to go anyway. Moral: ask. Make yourself visible. Ask the boat personnel. They seem to be the only ones who know what they are doing. They are nice and used to dealing with foreign tourists.

WHERE TO STAY

The one hotel on the island, Le Manoir (83400 Île de Port-Cros; tel. 94.05.90.52), is an elegant nineteenth-century manor house a short distance from the village. It is open from the beginning of May to the first week in October, with a choice of half-board or full-board, and will provide an ample picnic for hikers. They have a five-night mini-

mum stay in July and August and a three-night minimum in June and September. Expensive.

At the other end of the scale, L'Hostellerie de Provence, a restaurant at the port, has a few very simple rooms to rent at rock-bottom prices. Bring your own towel, soap, and so forth. Showers and toilet are down the hall. The energetic blond proprietor, Regine Anger, is delightful, and these rooms are available year-round. Madame Anger asks that you call ahead in winter and promises to dust off her schoolgirl English for you. The cost per room was 150F ($22) for two people in 1989. (Île de Port-Cros; 83400 Hyères; tel. 94.05.90.43.)

There are no camping facilities on the island; with the dry climate and limited water supply, the fire hazard is too great.

WHERE TO EAT

L'Hostellerie de Provence, the restaurant farthest to your right as you face the town, has an agreeable dining room overlooking the port which serves seafood specialties a bit on the pricey side. A pleasant touch is the bowl of dark, briny olives flavored with rosemary brought to you at the beginning of the meal. The owners, Regine and Philippe Anger, take their meals in the restaurant with their two school-age children. Monsieur Anger's family has been on the island for generations. Set-price meal at 125F ($20).

L'Anse du Port, at the extreme left side as you face the settlement from the port, is a big informal restaurant with excellent, unpretentious food. Again, the specialties are fish. It is cheaper than the Hostellerie, with a set-price menu at 90F ($15).

Le Manoir, the restaurant in the luxury hotel, has a set-price menu at 190F ($31).

None of the restaurants serve dinner before 8:00 p.m. There are a couple of cafés where you can get breakfast, drinks, or sandwiches. Avoid the one next to the Hostellerie; the prices are outrageous.

In the late afternoon, we sat in a harbor café trying to get the waiter to sort out the boat schedule with us. He was charming but not very well informed. Shortly, his friends came along with a heavy sack of silvery *boules* and started up a game in front of his establishment. In between customers, he joined them. They played for a couple of hours, swearing and teasing each other in the accent of the Midi as they tossed the balls in the dust. The loser bought drinks all around.

In the summer, there is a tiny grocery store on the back street behind the Hostellerie which is open mornings and late afternoons. Don't forget to take drinks and snacks on your walks; nothing is available outside the village.

Île du Levant

The third inhabited island in the chain is a strange coupling: seven-eighths of the island is a military installation, and the remainder is the site of the naturist colony, Héliopolis.

Founded in 1931 by two French doctors as a place where people could come to take simple, healthful vacations away from the city and "as close as possible to a state of nature," Héliopolis claims to be the first and oldest naturist colony in the world.

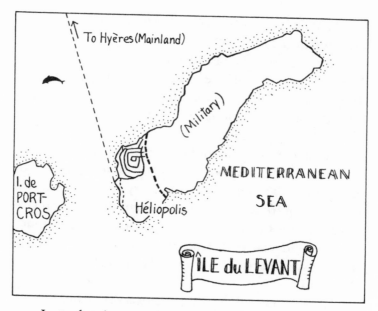

Just what *is* a naturist colony? Is everyone going to be prancing around naked in the streets? Will there be soldiers peering through the fence at naked ladies? Are we going to feel funny with our clothes on?

On a sunny weekend in late May, we saw hardly anyone, naked or clothed. You may see an occasional sunbather tripping along the cliffs or across the square in a towel or less, and the proprietor of one hotel did pull on his pants before greeting us at the reception desk. But you can get used to anything. Everyone is so kind and friendly that you won't feel embarrassed with or without clothes. People do dress in restaurants.

With so much nudity on French beaches already, you may wonder if a special place for it isn't a little redundant, a little *vieux jeu*? When we were there, the colony did seem frequented mostly by old-timers who had been coming there for years.

As you approach the island by boat, you see a long stretch of empty woodland (the military buildings are not visible from the water) with a colorful bunching of pink and white houses with red tile roofs scattered over the island's hilly end.

There is no natural harbor here; the lack of shelter from the wind makes docking too rough for pleasure boats. The only dock is a cement slab where the ferry ties up for its brief calls. An extremely steep road curves up around the settlement to the top, where the town square lies. A shuttle bus is timed with the arrival and departure of the boat. The fare for the brief ride is as steep (10F per person, 6F per suitcase) as the hill it goes up but worth it if you are loaded down with luggage on a hot day. For vigorous walkers, a stone stairway goes straight up from the port to the top of the hill.

The village of Héliopolis is a very small place that conveys, because of the military installation, a tightly circumscribed feeling. Streets and paths circle one end of the island like fingers gripping a knee. The village is cast over such steep slopes that strolling around these streets, you have incredible views of the sea in between rather haphazardly tended but charming houses and gardens. Everything here is slightly beat-up looking. The trees and buildings have withstood the mistral—the capricious Provençal wind—for many summers. There is color: oleander, geraniums, bougainvillea, everywhere you turn.

From the village square, a large flagstone hub with streets radiating from it, you can take the *parcours santé*

(health parcourse). This trail soon divides into "health parcourse" and "nature walk." Even if you have no intention
of doing the exercises prescribed on the signposts, follow
the health parcourse through the maquis to the top of the
hill, where you get a view down the entire length of the
island and military installation. If you continue to follow
the trail through the woods—it can be quite steep and slip-
pery with fallen oak leaves—you will come out on one of
the lower roads that circle through the residential area. Follow it until you reach the port.

On the other side of the port, walk along the rocky
wave-splashed path to a pretty but very tiny beach from
which you can look across the channel to the tip of Port-
Cros and the fort of Port-Man. There are also poured concrete platforms spaced intermittently along the rocks on

both sides of the port for sunbathers. You will see a sign at the beginning of the path to the beach, which says it is for nudists only.

HOW TO GET THERE

Some of the boats that go to Port-Cros from Hyères and Le Lavandou also stop at Île du Levant. Boats unload and load very quickly here. More than one person has been left stranded as they turned around to pick up the last suitcase. If one tries to take off without you, yell! They may pretend not to like it, but they'll probably come back.

WHERE TO STAY

Whether because of the regimented way the French think about vacations or because this spot is a little special, it is practically deserted off-season, leaving you your choice of inexpensive hotel rooms with flowery gardens and expansive views of the sea.

Hotel de la Brise Marine (83400 Île du Levant, Var, France; tel. 94.05.91.15, off-season tel. 94.71.69.44) is an idyllic place with charming cool gardens, two interior courtyards full of tile work, flowers, and a fountain. On the second floor, there is a flagstone terrace with a tiny swimming pool and a fabulous sea view. The dining room and many of the rooms also have views of the water. Friendly staff. Moderate.

Le Ponant (83400 Île du Levant; tel. 94.05.90.41) is a rather dreary hotel way down the hill, nearer to the port than the village. Overlooking the sea directly, the terraces here give the impression of being on the deck of a ship. The

owners are a Dutch woman who has lived in France for 30 years and her son. Restaurant. Inexpensive.

Au Minimum (83400 Île du Levant; tel. 94.05.91.78) is aptly described by its tongue-in-cheek name; this is a utilitarian place on the village square. Cheap. You can also rent cottages through this address.

Many of the hotels are closed off-season. Almost everything is closed during the winter, but you could probably just take the boat over and rent a room or a bungalow. This spot is not for everyone, but for the open-minded, budget-conscious traveler, it's a very special alternative. It has great weather year-round, and except for summer, this is an empty paradise.

WHERE TO EAT

All the hotels have restaurants; some require half-board. In addition, there is a scattering of simple restaurants serving rosemary-flavored grilled meats and garlicky southern French specialties.

Stop for lunch or a drink at Le Gambaro, a happy café overlooking the port. Just to show that these nudists don't take themselves too seriously, when we ordered a salad here, the chef insisted that he'd stood naked in front of the tomatoes so they would blush and turn red.

ITALY

Aeolians

At dusk, through the filmed-over windows of the hydrofoil, the islands of the Aeolian chain appear to be a row of charcoal lumps casually strewn in the sea. Near the north coast of Sicily, they look on the map to be a long drop down from Naples and even farther from the cities of northern Italy. But they are only four hours by hydrofoil from Naples, giving you the sense of having arrived in a very remote place in a very short time. Here, in contrast to many places in Italy, the water is clear, the strong Mediterranean light undiluted by air pollution, the streets free of raucous mainland traffic. Although these islands were once so poor that many of their inhabitants immigrated to Australia or the United States, the increased crowding and pollution of the Italian Riviera have made them a vacation refuge for Italians. In summer, northern Europeans also come, but in spring and fall, in "low season" to use the jargon of the hoteliers, there is only a smattering of tourists. Even in June, facilities are not even close to capacity. Fortunately, development is limited by strict controls on new construction, as the Italians recognize the value of preserving these peaceful, unspoiled places.

The seven islands of the chain are all very different from one another. The attraction of Stromboli is its volcano, Panarea its stunning beauty, Salina its peaceful, backwater charm. People are drawn to Vulcano for the mineral baths and to Alicudi and Filicudi for their remoteness. Lipari, with its bustling, touristy port and top-flight Etruscan museum, is the gateway to all the islands and the administrative capital for all but Salina, which has an autonomous administration.

There can be ferocious winds through these islands. According to the *Odyssey*, when Odysseus landed here, Aeolus, wind god and king of the islands, gave him a bag of wind to speed him home. Curious, he opened it, and the escaped wind pushed him right back into port.

If the scirocco isn't blowing too hard, you can take a trip around the island. If the Siremar office is open, you can find out when the ferry leaves. If the bank is open, you can change money. If there are enough people, the guide will go up the mountain. If the volcano is active, you'll see something besides smoke.

These notes about life on Stromboli reflect our experience in the entire Aeolian chain. This attitude prevails: if we can, we will, but if we can't, so what? Tomorrow the wind will stop blowing, the weather will change, the volcano may erupt. In a world of splendid weather and natural beauty that has also over the centuries endured poverty, natural disaster, and foreign invasions, the people we met knew how to live well from day to day and take what comes. What comes is often wonderful human connections, major and minor. Once we hung around the Siremar office for two days waiting for it to open so we could find out about boats. No hours were posted. "It's open when the boat comes," the woman at the hotel desk assured us. "Ask to Luigi." Finally, the extremely charming hotel manager called Luigi at home. No problem, we could easily have an overnight cabin from Lipari to Naples. "And is there a place on the docks in Lipari where we can check our bags while we visit the Etruscan museum?" we asked the manager. "One moment." He scribbled something on the back of his card. "Give this to the man who runs the newspaper stand at the port. He'll keep it for you. He's a friend of mine." Dare we generalize? Is this the way things work in Sicily? Relationship is all.

HOW TO GET THERE

The word for hydrofoil in Italian is *aliscafi*; a bus is called a *Pullman*.

Except in winter, ferries and hydrofoils crisscross between the seven Aeolian islands, Naples, and several points on Sicily several times a day; even the locals are astonished at their frequency, which has doubled in the last couple of years. Service is competitive among three companies:

SNAV (only hydrofoils), Via Caracciolo 10, Naples; tel. 081/7612348

SIREMAR (hydrofoils and ferries), Via Francesco Crispi, Palermo; tel. 091/582688

COVEMAR (hydrofoils and ferries), Mole Beverello, Naples; tel. 081/5515384

The addresses and phone numbers above are for the regional offices. They are often busy all day. In addition, each company has a little office or kiosk at the port of call where tickets are sold and schedules are available. They are often open only around arrival and departure times of the boats, although they leave schedules posted outside. The boat company offices are usually located side by side but open at different times. Don't expect to get information about one company's schedule or rates from another company. You might try to get a published schedule from each company to use while you are traveling around, but remember that there may be additional boats; the schedules are only printed once a year. Boats *are* frequent between the islands, often three or four times a day, more in summer. Rule of thumb: *The closer you get to where you are going, the easier it is to get information about boats, so do not try to plan your itinerary too carefully ahead of time.*

In Naples, hydrofoil departures are from one pier, Mole Merghillina, and ferries from another, Mole Beverello, a short bus or taxi ride away. At Merghillina, there is a place to check your bags on the pier if you get there early. Don't make your connections too close together if you're island hopping. Despite their sleek and swift appearance, these hydrofoils can be delayed for unexplained reasons, even in summer.

The ferry from the islands to Naples pokes along very gently so as to make the journey last all night, putting you in Naples early in the morning. You can reserve space in a two-bunk cabin. First class is roomier and correspondingly more expensive. The boat calls at several islands, the last being Stromboli, where there is a layover from 8:00 to 10:00 in the evening. Plan to have dinner on the island; the quality of the food in the ship's dining room is not high.

There are private coaches to Rome (Piazza Indipendenza) which coordinate with the ferries to Naples. You can buy tickets on the ferry or before boarding the bus. These are slightly more expensive than the train, but they are very efficient and save you the trip from the pier to the train station.

The hydrofoils are much quicker than the ferries. Traveling on them is rather like being in a plane over the Rockies when the weather is iffy. You will probably choose between hydrofoil and ferry according to which departure times fit your schedule the best, but the ferries are cheaper and more leisurely and allow you to stay out on the deck and get much better views of the coastal scenery. The ferries also carry cars. Sample one-way fares in 1989:

Ferry Naples-Lipari, L41,300 ($26)
Ferry Stromboli-Panarea, L5,100 ($3)
Hydrofoil Naples-Stromboli, L74,000 ($46)
Hydrofoil Salina-Lipari, L6,600 ($4)

In addition to the multiple connections from Naples, boat travel is possible to the Aeolian islands from the following points in Sicily and Calabria: Milazzo, Palermo, Cefalu, Messina, Reggio Calabria, Vibo Valentia, and Capo D'Orlando.

From Lipari, in addition to the regularly scheduled ferries and hydrofoils, there are excursion boats that make day trips to one or more of the other islands, often including times for a swim at the beach or a stop at a particularly fine grotto.

Lipari

Although not one of our undiscovered islands, Lipari, the Aeolian capital, is worth a visit for the Etruscan museum alone. A bustling port town, it is divided into two parts: the café-lined Marina Corta, which is the hydrofoil port, and Marina Lunga, where the ferries dock. Between them is a hill on which the old castle and the Etruscan museum are located.

The site of the Castello has been inhabited since 3000 B.C. and is the source of many of the archaeological finds that fill the Etruscan museum. The location of the digs is still visible and clearly marked to show the remains of the various civilizations—Bronze Age, Ausonian, Greek, and so on—layered on top of one another over the centuries. Inside, the exhibits are arranged chronologically and clearly labeled so that even if you don't read Italian you can follow the progression from room to room, from early polished obsidian objects to potsherds and amphorae bearing Minoan and Greek design to perfectly preserved Greek vases and sculpture. Particularly exquisite are the tiny masks in Room XXI representing characters from comedies and tragedies by Sophocles and Euripides. Some of the pots are exhibited in the museum exactly as they were found encased in dirt or sunk into walls of stone. The collection is housed in two buildings; do not miss the second section, which is much more interesting. The museum is open daily from 9:00 a.m. to 2:00 p.m. and on holidays from 9:00 a.m. to 1:00 p.m. Admission is free.

Next to the Castello is the baroque church of San Bartholomeo, with its fine old bell. There is also a youth hostel on the hilltop.

Stromboli

Farthest west in the Aeolian chain is Stromboli. From a distance, it looks like a toy volcano with imitation smoke. The island is a soft gray in the evening mist, like a Monet painting. As you approach, the white village becomes distinct, looking as stark and straight as some old New England port. Dominating the town is the flat yellow facade of the church, broken by white painted pillars; a little farther along stands its small replica in rose. Halfway up, the mountain is encircled by a yellow wreath of scotch broom; from there to the top is a cone of fine volcanic dust.

The boats dock at the beach at Fico Grande (Big Fig). Here little three-wheel vehicles with awnings (each hotel has one) will haul you and your luggage up the long beachfront road to the village, along a lengthy stretch of black sand beach, past the low rectangular white houses built in the Aeolian style, with porthole windows and plain round columns, and always, in the near distance, *il volcano*.

STROMBOLI
VULCANO CON ATTIVITA' ESPLOSIVA

SALIRE SUL CRATERE SOLO CON GUIDA AUTORIZZATA
DO NOT CLIMB VULCANO WITHOUT AUTORIZED GUIDE
NE MONTER AU CRATERE QU'AVEC GUIDE AUTORISE
NUR IN BEGLEITUNG EINES ANERKANNTEN FÜHRER DEN KRATER BESTEIGEN

The volcano, one of the few continuously active in the world, *is* the island and determines its life. Strombolians interrogate it as if it were a person. "Hey there," they ask, using the familiar Italian *tu* form, "are you sleeping today or what?" People come to see it, to climb it, or to lounge on the black sand beaches at its base.

If you want to climb to the top of the volcano, gather in front of the sign on the beach near the Sirenetta hotel at Fico Grande around 5:00 p.m. One of the two guides,

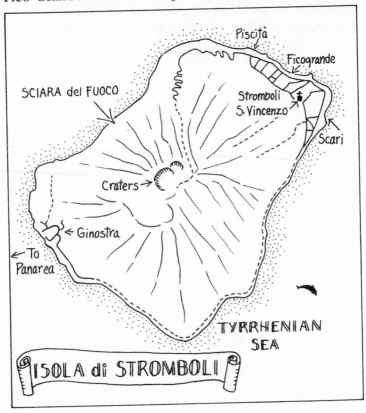

Tonio or Nino, will take you up if there are enough people. In 1989, the going rate was L15,000 per person. If there are fewer than ten people, the rate goes up to L22,000 per person. It's well worth the price for five or six hours of the guide's attention and expertise. Sturdy shoes, a flashlight, and a warm sweater are required; a day pack or shoulder bag is also advisable so your hands are free to grab onto rocks. There is a good trail for most of the climb, but there is a tricky stretch at the top where you have to scramble a bit.

This climb is not for the faint-hearted. The pace is rapid, up 3,000 feet in three hours, and for the last stretch you slog through lava dust up to your ankles. If you have the stamina, it is definitely worth the effort. The volcano varies from active to less active; the night we went it was quiet, but we could still look down into the crater and see flares of pink flowering through the smoke. On more active days, the lava bubbles over and tumbles straight down the mountain into the sea.

When the volcano is active, you can take excursions by boat at night to the Sciara del Fuoco and view the pour of lava from the water. If you don't want to make the climb or the boat trip, the volcano action can best be seen from land at a plaza in front of St. Vincent's church known as the Observatory.

There are other activities on Stromboli besides volcano watching. If water sports tempt you, there is plenty to do. The Sirenetta hotel operates its own diving school. A little farther up the road, there is a windsurfing school, and kayaks, catamarans, and motorboats are all available for rental on the beach.

Also on the beach at Fico Grande are boats that make daily excursions around the island, weather and sufficient clientele permitting. Just hang out at the beach around 10:00 a.m., looking for the boats marked GITE DEL ISOLA. The going rate is L15,000 per person. The boats pass close to Strombolicchio, the tiny offshore island shaped by the scirocco to look like a peaky castle. Going around the island, you can see several places where streams of lava have scored the face of the rocks.

The boat trip includes a half hour stop at Ginostra, the isolated village on the other side of the mountain. Here it is possible to dock two boats side by side in the tiny port when the weather is not too rough. You can walk up the steep switchback road. All transportation here is by donkey; there are no cars or motorbikes. The village seems very remote, but there are daily hydrofoils and ferries from here to Panarea.

Try not to take the Gita del Isola on a day of *mare brut-to* (rough sea) or you may "suffer the sea," as the charming translation goes. An alternative is to take the Siremar ferry to Panarea. It stops at Ginostra, so you get at least halfway around the island. With luck, you will get to watch the rowboat come out and maneuver passengers and freight onto the big boat. The smiling, bare-chested boatmen know they are colorful and like to ham it up.

WHERE TO STAY

La Sirenetta (Via Marina 33, 98050 Stromboli; tel. 090/986025-986062) is a modern hotel with very pretty little rooms in white plastered bungalows. It has a swimming pool and is across from beach. Very pleasant staff, some English-speaking, and a good dining room. Moderate. Half-pension is required.

La Sciara Residence (98050 Stromboli; tel 090/986004 or 986005) is a large modern hotel with a pool and a beautiful garden, a little more formal than La Sirenetta. Half-board is required. Expensive.

Pension Villa Petrusa (98050 Stromboli; tel. 090/986045) has very basic room and board with sea views. Management is pleasant. Inexpensive.

Most hotels require half-board. In addition, there is a scattering of trattorias in the village.

From Linda's journal after climbing the volcano: Toward the end of our climb, the air chills. We have lost almost all of our light. For the last 50 meters of the 1,000-meter ascent we tramp straight up through fine lava dust up to our ankles, slopes falling steeply away to either side. I remember the turgid melodrama—Ingrid Bergman in Roberto Rossellini's *Stromboli*, dragging herself over the mountain through the smoke and dust. Little did I know.

Finally, three hours after our departure, we are at the summit, walking easily along the ridge. Overhead hangs a rosy half moon, and below, a pool of sulfurous smoke covers the soup of fire, hidden tonight, that still flares and spits enough for a glimpse of pulsing pink through a skin of smoke.

From this moonscape, we can see the distant lights of Milazzo, on Sicily. As we huddle together, shivering, I feel more and more included in this clutch of exhilarated Italian hikers.

The sharp wind not only pierces the several layers of clothing we are now each wearing but also blows gritty smoke in our faces. Someone asks the guide how long we will stay. "We usually stay an hour," he replies. Is it obligatory? Everyone laughs with relief as we prepare to leave, testing flashlights, adjusting packs.

The climb up was hard enough in daylight. I wonder how we will ever get down, especially the 50 meters or so where we had to toe test everything before trusting the rocks to hold. Then we are flying crazily full tilt down a different trail, shoes filling with volcanic dust, steep slopes falling away on either side, laughing, going too fast to stop, a mad ballet lit by the moon glowing through the craggy rocks behind us and by our dancing flashlights.

We take turns warning each other about upcoming pitfalls—steep steps, overhanging branches, arroyos. I share my flashlight with someone whose batteries went out. Exhausted and slightly hysterical as we all are now, there is no language barrier; I understand Italian perfectly, as my companions do English. We have silly in-jokes; we are eternal friends.

After two or three hours of this, we hit the paved streets of the village and immediately take our hot, tender feet out of our shoes and shake the dust out of them. The pavement is soothingly rough and warm. Some of us wander into a café for a beer, others drift home in the moonlight. "Wait," I want to say, "what about tomorrow? Isn't there something else we could climb?"

Panarea

Panarea, smallest of the Aeolian islands, is also the most chic. It is the "fiora all' occhiello," flower in the lapel, of the chain. Thirty years ago, Panarea was so poor that many of its residents deserted to Brooklyn or Perth; now their abandoned houses have been carefully restored as vacation homes for well-off fugitives from Rome, Turin, and Milan. Some of the wealthiest Italian industrialists have hideaways here. This is not immediately apparent since there is no new construction, no ostentation. However, the beautifully kept, whitewashed houses adorned with bougainvillea and other vines, the high walls, the absence of tourist shlock, the pricey shops with bright trendy clothes give it away: there's money here.

There used to be three settlements here; you were delivered by small boat to the one of your choice. Since the construction of the concrete pier, all activity is centered at the port of San Pietro. Its back streets are full of shops, trattorias, and *locandas*; steps and old donkey paths wind around clusters of attractive houses. Most of the houses are white, but a few of the unrestored ones retain their faded pinks and yellows, colors of Pompeii. Two streets, broad but not broad enough for cars, wing out from the village in either direction, one toward the beach and old settlement at Cala Junco, the other up the hill to the old Calcara, or hot springs. The far side of the island is inaccessible by land; the inhabited stretch backs up against the sere, rust-colored, cactus-covered mountains.

To get to the beach at Cala Junco, walk up past the Hotel Raya at the south end of San Pietro. When you come to a fork, go to the left for the beach. The walk out here is simply gorgeous, not to be missed. Stay on this road until it ends. On one side, you have a steady view of the sea; on the other, the craggy, cactus-covered, rusty pink mountains, and all along the way, the square, bright white, Aeolian houses with their plain archways, tiny porthole windows, and squatty, stolid pillars. Here and there, you will spot a shapely old amphora planted with ivy geranium. There is bougainvillea everywhere, the electronic hum of cicadas, and behind the walled gardens, the musical rise and fall of the most beautiful language in the world.

At the end of the road, there is a splendid little bay and a pleasant beach with good swimming. There are two nearby trattorias in case you have forgotten your picnic.

At Punta Milazzese, on the cliffs beyond the beach, are

the remains of an ancient settlement belonging to a pre-Bronze Age religious cult. There is no literature available in Panarea on this bit of archaeology, not even a sign indicating how to get there. On the far side of the beach, you will see a path heading up into the cliffs which looks as if it dis-

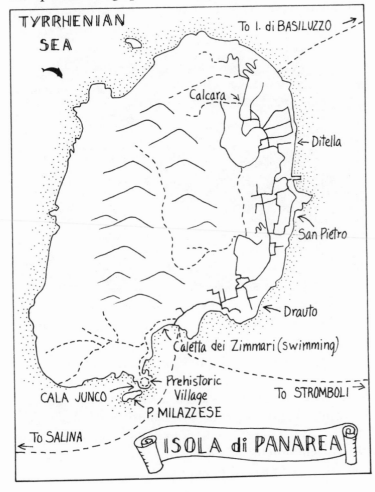

appears and you will have to scramble to the top. In fact, there is a broad stone path all the way up that makes this an easy climb. When you reach the top, follow the stone staircase out onto the little spit of land where you will see a series of stone circles that once were the foundations of houses in the settlement. Be sure to walk to the far end of

the spit and peer down into the calm dark blue grottoes on the other side. Now look behind you at wall after wall of stone terraces that striate the mountain, monument to the centuries of labor once poured into this spare, rocky place.

To reach the spot known as Calcara, walk out of town the other direction until you see a whitewashed sign on a stone pointing to ''Calcara,'' then follow the long, rocky road all the way down to the water. Here there is the faint smell of sulfur in the breeze but no inviting-looking warm pool to sit in. In fact, the water looks rather rough. However, in the early evening the sunlight is golden on the huge pink rocks, and across the water sit two little peaky uninhabited islands that looks almost like stalagmites. When we were there, two men in a rubber raft had been fishing and were having trouble starting up their motor. A sailboat appeared and was gone. Away from the cafés, the hydrofoils, the port, it was timeless and peaceful. We half expected some benevolent goddess to rise up out of the sea.

Panarea has its own collection of offshore rocks and islets, such as those at Calcara. The most notable is Basiluzzo, where there are traces of Roman habitation. There are excursions by boat during the summer.

If you are on a limited budget, do not be put off by Panarea's chic side. It is easy to find inexpensive rooms and meals here, and it is our choice for most beautiful spot in this island chain. Panarea is a place to come and do nothing. Ignore the beautiful people or join them, in summer, at the Hotel Raya's disco. Take a stroll or a boat excursion, or just sit in a café at the port and watch the tourists come and go and the water boat from Trapani rise in the water as it unloads the island's supply.

WHERE TO STAY

Off-season, it is easy to get cheap rooms in locandas in Panarea. The Stella Maris, on the port, is a good example, although their restaurant is to be avoided. Hotel Cincotta (98050 Panarea, tel. 090/983014 or 983015; PBX 983001) has a beautiful garden and sea views. Moderate. Half-board is required except during the off-season.

The expensive and rather glamorous Hotel Raya (98050

Panarea, Isole Eolie, Sicily; tel. 090/983013-983029; fax 983103) has its office, restaurant, bar, disco, and shops overlooking the port, but its rooms are located in a pink and white multilayered structure flung up against the hillside behind the village. There is no sign or indication that it is a hotel. It was built to harmonize with the indigenous architecture by an Egyptian, Paolo Tilche, who has lived on Panarea for thirty years and has done much to bring about the preservation and restoration of the island's architectural style. The hotel is very quiet, with a large garden of native plants. They do not accept children. Half-board is required but flexible; for example, you can skip dinner one night and bring a friend the next. Admission to the disco, normally L25,000 ($15), is free to hotel guests.

WHERE TO EAT

The restaurant at the Hotel Raya, with its white arches outlining sea and stars, is quite stunning, and the food is good. The night we were there, the menu included a heavenly risotto with radicchio and a rich mascarpone cheese and fish baked in salt. You can eat here without being a hotel guest, but reservations are usually needed. At the end of the beach road, Il Nuncio overlooks the bay; Trattoria La Sirena is a little way up the road. Three restaurants at the port have wonderful views of the bay.

Salina

"Panarea e troppo sofisticata."
                    —Catena da Pasquale, resident of Salina
"Salina is decrepit and melancholy. There is nothing there."
          —Paolo Tilche, owner of the Hotel Raya, Panarea

Salina is Italy unselfconscious, Italy left behind. Houses have
been abandoned by people who emigrated to America or Australia and died; they cannot be sold. The town of San Marino has one long dusty street with a couple of shops selling
old film and one or two grocery stores and produce shops.
An old woman sits in front of her house shelling garbanzo
beans, an old man zips up his pants on the balcony after his
afternoon nap. The young village idiot (so he was described
to us) hangs around wearing a T-shirt inscribed in English
"once is never enough." On a terrace that also serves as an
outdoor kitchen, a grandmother fastens and refastens the bar-
rette in her four-year-old granddaughter's hair. The child tugs
at her skirt and smiles at the photographer, a French woman
who looks like Simone Signoret and has lived in Sicily for
twenty years. Posing completed, the grandmother pours the
visitors a shot of orange liqueur she has made herself.

The grandmother and her husband are worried. They
have lived in this house for years, but the owner is going to
sell it. Houses here are just beginning to be bought and
restored as summer homes. The air is just as clear here, the
sea as beautiful, as on the more touristy islands. And for now,
real estate is cheaper. A few tourists come, mostly young Germans on a budget who like to hike and swim.

Catena de Pasquale lets rooms and little apartments in

her home. Another nephew, Franco, owns the best restaurant around. Patricia, another relative, owns another restaurant, Mamma Santini's. You can phone Catena to get in touch with another relative, Alberto Cincotta, who will guide you up the mountain, or *felche*. Or you can go to la Cambusa, the café at the port, and ask for him. He's usually around there. Catena's nephew, Ricardo Gullo, is the mayor. He is a bearded, soulful-looking man in a T-shirt with a crucifix over his desk. He is also the town's first communist *sindago*. If there is a contradiction here, nobody notices.

Salina is big, green, mountainous, and undeveloped. It is green because it has been planted with eucalyptus and

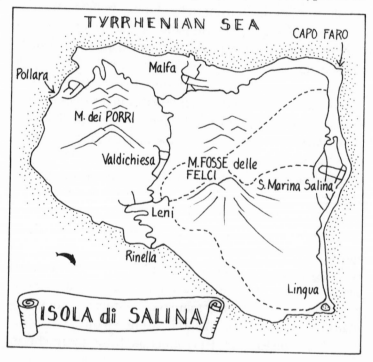

pine, which are not native to the region. It is undeveloped for tourism because there is no money for it, and because of a kind of sweet indifference that comes from fear, inferiority, or failure of imagination. When Ricardo Gullo predicts a pleasure port in Santa Marina in four years, you get the feeling he has just made it up for the press.

Unlike most of the other Aeolian islands, there is still agriculture on Salina. The sweet wine called *malvasia* is produced, and capers continue to be gathered here, although this happens less and less as the pay is a little over a dollar a kilo for many hours of intense work. The caper is the bud of an orchidlike flower, which blooms all over the island.

A road goes from one side of the island to the other over the mountain and connects the island's seven small communities. From Lingua, where the wine cooperative is located, through Santa Marina, the local bus wends its way up the tortuous, flower-lined mountain road to Capo Faro, where there is a lighthouse and a tiny village overlooking the sea. From there, the route continues to Malfa, where a couple of pleasant, reasonably priced hotels are perched on the cliffs, and stairs lead down to a rocky beach with good swimming. Malfa has a couple of restaurants and the island's only bank, the Aetna, open all year from 9:00 a.m. to 2:00 p.m. only. From here, the road splits; first, the bus drops down to the sleepy village of Pollara, and then, it goes back up and down the other side of the mountain.

At Pollara it is a steep climb down from the village to the large, deeply scooped out bay, a volcanic crater, where you can lie on the beach or swim looking up at sheer black walls. Caves cut into the rock serve as splendid stone boathouses for the local fishermen. To the right of the bay, you can make your way around the rocks past the boathouses to view a magnificent outcropping of rock with a huge stone archway through which you can see Panarea and Stromboli on a clear day. Take the bus up in the early morning (with picnic and water; there are no shops in Pollara) and spend the day.

From Pollara, the bus winds back up and across the island between the two dormant volcanoes, M. Dei Porri and M. Fossa delle Felci. This road passes through two tiny communities. Valdichiesa, once thickly forested, was a refuge for persecuted monks in the time of the late Roman Empire and the Vandals. Here the Virgin was prayed to and a chapel was constructed in the sixth century. In the seventeenth century, with the renewal of the cult of the Virgin, the Sanctuary of the Madonna del Terzito was built. It is a plain, tan, twin-spired church where the nuns run a hospice for old people. Farther down the mountain is Leni, the agricultural center of the island (the name comes from the Greek *lenoi*, which means tubs for pressing wine), and from here, the road drops quickly and sharply down to Rinella, with its single café, trattoria, church, and tiny port.

One day, we watched the vegetable cart pull up in front of the café in Rinella. (How quickly one begins to take for granted the existence of the fruit and vegetable truck!) The café cook came out, the barman, the woman in the postcard shop. Four grown men spent ten minutes discussing tomatoes.

This is a pleasant, *very quiet* place to watch the ferries and aliscafis come in, which they do with astonishing frequency. It is possible to rent undersea equipment from the little diving shop there.

HOW TO GET THERE

There are daily frequent departures from Lipari to both Rinella and Santa Marina. You can also reach the island directly from Milazzo and Messina, on Sicily. Local buses coordinate with boat arrivals.

If you are traveling in Italy by car, this is one island worth bringing it to. It has more roads and greater distances than others in the chain.

A bus schedule can be read in the boat ticket offices. Just because there is a schedule does not always mean there is a bus, however. They *usually* come, and when they do, they cover the island very efficiently, even though the driver who plies this route is so cross-eyed, it is hard to know how he negotiates those hairpin turns. He knows everyone on the line and jokes with them and is very patient with tourists.

WHERE TO STAY

We came into San Marino without a reservation. Our guidebook told us there were five one-star hotels along the port. Where did they go? We found a place with rooms to let and tumbled into the bosom of a Sicilian family. Catena de Pasquale rents very inexpensive rooms and apartments with pretty little terraces and outdoor kitchens all year. In summer, call for a reservation (tel. 090/9843094). One of her daughters speaks English.

In Malfa, Punta Scario (Via Scalo, tel. 090/9844139) overlooks the sea. It is moderately priced. In Rinella, L'Ariana, also moderately priced, has a beautiful terrace restaurant overlooking the harbor. The Hotel Villaggio at Capo Faro has a pool and tennis courtyards amid the vineyards, but it is far from the towns. It, too, is moderately priced.

WHERE TO EAT

Ristorante Da Franco, up a back street in Santa Marina (no address, ask the locals), is the best restaurant on the island. There is almost always fresh fish and whatever else Franco has made that day. There is a pretty terrace with a view and excellent service by Franco's young wife and a son who is a carbon copy of his serious father.

Mamma Santini's restaurant, also in Santa Marina, has been taken over by her daughter Patricia and her husband, who serve simple food in an attractive, open-walled room and have a few rooms to rent. Follow the signs off of the main street up the hill.

In Sciavo's grocery store (*alimentari*) in Santa Marina, we ordered a sandwich made with fresh mozzarella and prosciutto, drizzled with olive oil and sprinkled with oregano. Fantastic.

Giglio

This charming five-by-thirteen-mile island off the coast of Tuscany, near Elba, is a fine place to spend a few days if you are traveling on the Italian coast. It was once a prosperous agricultural community, but since the island has become a getaway spot for Italians from nearby cities, agriculture has been neglected for the more lucrative business of tourism.

Like Gaul, Giglio is divided into three parts: Giglio Porto, the pretty, crescent-shaped harbor town; Giglio Castello, the walled medieval town at the top of the hill; and Campese, the sleepy beach community on the far side of the island.

All boats arrive at Giglio Porto. This is a place to relax, stroll the waterfront and the jetty, and admire the multicolored facades and the peeling painted wrought-iron balconies. You can spend hours under a grape arbor in a dockside café or wander under the archways and alleys of the back streets, peering into dahlia-filled gardens with their substantial stonework. On the street that leads up to the simple village church, there are a couple of boutiques and a post office. Other souvenir shops and restaurants dot the harbor; one shop has some pretty painted pottery.

If you take the 10:00 a.m. bus from Giglio Porto up the mountain to Giglio Castello (it coordinates with the arrival of the ferry), it will put you in the medieval walled town just as the shops are starting to open. At this hour women are leaving home with their shopping bags, and shopkeepers are setting out their displays. The castle itself was closed for renovation when we were there in 1989, but that didn't detract from the delicious pleasure of winding around the narrow stone streets that lead up to it, ducking under archways made for the much shorter Italians of long ago. The exterior stairways and balconies decked with tumbling ivy geranium and succulents make a photographer's paradise.

As you walk around the harbor and the walled town,

you will notice one of the most appealing aspects of the island—the way the local residents greet each other cordially and formally every morning and stop to chat or peer into a baby carriage as they pass each other on their way somewhere. These are families who have known each other for generations.

Like so many Mediterranean islands, Giglio has a long history of attack from North African pirates. In 1544, Barbarossa abducted and enslaved more than 700 people, more than half the population. This makes you appreciate why the walled castle town is so heavily fortified.

The bus from Giglio Porto continues to Campese. This ride over the mountain is one of the island's treats; the steep switchback road gives you fabulous views of the sea and a long look at the old, carefully terraced vineyards and olive groves, the work of centuries now abandoned. Little round stone huts that must have sheltered the peasants from the noonday sun still dot the mountain slopes. Extroverted school kids getting on and off this bus show off for the tourists, delightfully.

In case you are tempted to hoof it up or over the mountain, we do not recommend this road for foot travel. It is very narrow and has no sidewalks or shoulder. Also, there are a lot of diesel fumes to chew.

Campese is a long, sleepy strip of dusty beach with a few hotels and a scattering of new apartments for summer rental. At one end of the beach is a wind-sheltered cove and an old stone tower; from there, you can walk out on the rocks to find a quiet, private place to sit and watch the water. Umbrellas, lounge chairs, and pedal boats can be rented on the beach. At one end of the bay stands a fine old stone

watchtower erected by Ferdinand I, Grand Duke of Tuscany.

In addition to the beach at Campese, there are several beaches accessible on foot from Giglio Porto. It is also possible to rent a small boat to explore hidden beaches and coves from the water.

The world turns around the comings and goings of the Giglio ferry. We left the island at 6:55 a.m., surrounded by the smell of strong coffee, brioche, and diesel oil. Baby, mother, and grandmother waved good-bye to great-grandmother. The sun fell on the soft, fading colors of the buildings. In back of the village rose the rocky mountain covered with macchia, the low underbrush. It was lovely and we were sorry to leave.

HOW TO GET THERE

From Rome Termini, take the train to Orbetello, a trip of almost two hours. Walk across the tracks and into the tiny train station. The bus to Porto San Stefano, from where the ferries depart, is coordinated with the train and will be waiting for you. Buy a bus ticket at the magazine stand in the train station (L1,800). The bus ride takes about 20 minutes.

You can also take a ferry from Genoa to Porto San Stefano. There are two competing ferry boat companies with offices side by side at the port. Each runs three or four boats a day to the island. If you have to wait for the boat, there is a shady café across the street. These boats are the cleanest we saw in Italy; the crew is constantly scrubbing and swabbing. As the boat leaves the harbor, you'll have a pretty view of the sandy cliffs of Porto San Stefano, the ocher facades of the waterfront houses drenched with light.

It's possible to take a car to Giglio, but why? The few cars on Giglio are belched off the ferry and go roaring up the streets as if the drivers were in Rome trying to get to work on time. Why add to the noise and air pollution, so far quite limited? A bus plies the windy road from one side of the island to the other frequently and dependably.

WHERE TO STAY

Campese: Giardino della Palme (58012 Isola del Giglio, Campese [GR]; tel. 0564/804037) is at the north end of beach, near the old tower. It has two shady terraces and a tennis court. Very quiet. Moderate.

Giglio Porto: Hotel Monticello (58013 Isola del Giglio; tel. 0564/809252 or 809238) is located on a hill above the town in an old castle. It offers pension with half-board or full board, a tennis court, and a pool. Moderate. The oldest hotel on Giglio is La Pergola (0564/809051), with seven clean modern rooms all overlooking the harbor. Do not be deceived by the gray, peeling facade; this is really very nice. It is owned by Signora Maria Cavero, whose father owned it before her. Moderate. The owners of the Bar Pierini in Giglio Porto have a couple of apartments that they rent to tourists. On a weekend in late May, they were both available without a reservation. Inquire at the bar.

WHERE TO EAT

Giglio Porto: There are two or three restaurants that are simply glass rooms built right out over the water; the waiters have to cross the street to the kitchen to order and fetch your dinner. Fare is simple, fish the specialty. Next to La Pergola at one end of the harbor is a trattoria called La Vecchia Pergola.

Giglio Castello: There is one tiny, delightful restaurant in this warren of streets and another larger, fancier one on the main square where the bus arrives.

Campese: There are a couple of trattorias and pizzerias and a large restaurant overlooking the water.

Procida

Procida, the smallest of the islands of the Gulf of Naples, lies west of Naples between its larger neighbor, Ischia, and the mainland promontory of Pozzuola, which closes off the bay at its northwestern end. The mainland is clearly visible only a few miles across the water from Procida's main port. Epomeo, Ischia's extinct volcano, rests quietly only a few miles to the southeast, off Procida's third port at Chiaiolella.

Perhaps because it is the smallest and the closest to the shore, Procida has been overlooked by most tourists and developers. The island cannot offer the thermal spas that have made Ischia famous, nor the drama of Capri's cliffs and glittering social scene. What it does offer, however, is a chance to experience the traditional, untainted character of a Neapolitan community. It is almost as if a piece of the neighborhoods of Naples broke away from the mainland twenty years ago and floated out here into the bay where time stopped. Here, if you look in the doorways, you see elderly ladies making lace, a bakery where loaves are still baked in a wood-burning oven, a barbershop with all the original furnishings. Baskets drop down from third-floor balconies on ropes, carrying a few thousand-lire notes on the way down and several eggplants or a loaf of bread on the way up. Men gather around as a fishing boat comes in to see what the catch has been that day; others sit along the waterfront mending their nets.

The noises are still those of Naples years ago, the clop-clop of the fishermen's wooden sandals on the stone pavement and the singsong call of the street vendor. Sunday is

the day to see city Neapolitans on holiday, family and picnic basket in tow. Except for middle-class Neapolitans and
a few young German campers, the island has been overlooked by the outside world, which flocks to her larger
neighbors.

The island economy is still based on the land and the
sea. There are vineyards and citrus groves in every backyard.
Procida is famous for its lemons. Backyard tomato patches
are as big as farms. The island's several nautical schools
demonstrate its long-standing tradition of seamanship. A

tradition that still survives, though just barely, is lacework, a cottage industry maintained by the women while they were waiting for their men to return from the sea.

Procida has many rituals associated with the sea and considerable folklore referring to the Penelopean patience, or lack of it, of Procidan women. These women were the inspiration for French writer Lamartine's nineteenth-century novel, *Graziella*. This name appears often on restaurants and businesses.

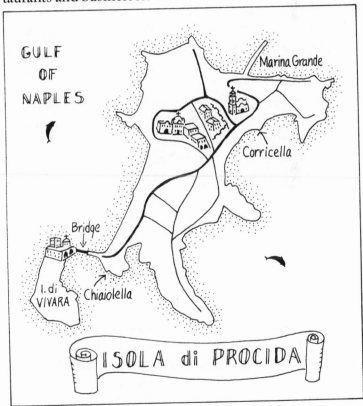

The island is not necessarily the one to choose for a week-long holiday at the sea, but it is certainly well worth a visit, either for an easy day's excursion from Naples or a weekend jaunt.

Marina Grande, the island's main harbor, is divided into two parts. The business end, where the ferries and hydrofoils arrive, is called Marina di San Cattolico. Here you will find only a couple of cafés. (The one with the red and white awning has a barman who speaks a little English and sells heavenly warm, flaky, jam-filled croissants.) At the other end of the harbor is the Marina Grande, which is filled with pleasure boats and sprawling outdoor restaurants with menus in German and English. This end of the port is a little less noisy and raucous. The two are divided by the big baroque church of Santa Maria della Pietà, whose bells peal out over a loudspeaker on the hour and at noon.

The center of town is located up the hill from the port and is easy to miss. Here is a village a bit more turned in on itself, not quite so oriented to the comings and goings of the boats. People chat around the little carts that hold the day's fresh catch of fish, and old women peer into baby carriages pushed by young mothers out shopping or going to the post office.

From the church of Santa Maria della Pietà, a steep street leads up through the town of Corricella to the top of the hill, where the Abbaye of San Michele is located. Half-way up you will come to the Piazza dei Martiri, a small square with a fine view of the bay, which has a monument listing the names of twelve Procidans executed by the Bourbons in 1799, when the island was occupied by the French. Continue to the walled city (Terra Murata) at the

top of the hill. Here you will be able to rest on a bench on a lovely stone terrace looking down on island rooftops and softly curving bays. This is the most spectacular spot on the whole island.

The road curves around from here to a stairway climbing up to the old walled town that surrounds the abbey. Simple enamel plaques mark the stations of the cross. At the top, spiral around the streets until you reach the very center, where you will find the simple yellow facade of the monastery. The main door of the church will probably be locked, but if you ring the bell to the green side door between 9:00 a.m. and noon or 1:00 and 4:00 p.m., the friendly priest will let you in and you can walk around the baroque interior. Here is kept the seventeenth-century silver statue of St. Michael the Archangel that is carried through the streets in procession on the feast day of the saint. On the ceiling, a painting by Luca Giordano depicts the saint fighting with Lucifer. You can ask the priest for the key to the library and catacombs downstairs, where you will find a couple of rooms full of books that look like they would powder if you touched them and a few skulls laid on an altar. This was a Benedectine monastery built in the eleventh century. The fortifications were built in the fourteenth century to protect it (unsuccessfully) from the island's various invaders. Barbarossa burned the church in 1544; it was reconstructed with income from the fishermen, who were given a special dispensation from the pope to work on Sundays to raise the money.

Return to the Piazza dei Martiri and go down to Corricella by way of a staircase that begins from the church of San Rocco. Corricella is the best place to contract with a fisherman to take you for a ride around the island. There are a few organized departures for a "giro dell' isola" by boat, but they only operate regularly on the weekend and during holidays. Information can be obtained from the tourist office at Marina Grande or at Agenzi Graziella, also Marina Grande but back behind the bus stop. Departures are from Chiaiolella and cost around L20,000 ($12) per person. One leaves at 10:15 a.m. and returns at 1:30 p.m., making a circle around the island with stops for a swim in several spots. The other excursion is a night trip to view the marine floor and includes a sampling of local wine and fish. Departure is at 9:30 p.m., returning at midnight. None of these excursions can accommodate a large number of people. Most passengers will probably be Italian families over from Naples for the day.

Near the ferry/hydrofoil dock at Marina Grande is a little square where the bus begins its run across to the other side of the island at Chiaiolella. The taxi stand is also located in this square. As the bus runs only along a limited route, you might opt to hire a "micro-taxi" for a little orientation tour. These are really converted "Ape" (bee) trucks, Fiat's miniature version of a pickup truck, with three wheels and handlebars! The micro-taxis have colorful plastic awnings with two padded benches in the back to accommodate passengers. Some of the more verbose drivers will not only tell you about the various parts of the island but also share a bit of the poetic philosophy peculiar to Neapolitans.

Crossing the island is an adventure in itself. The long narrow walled street snaking from one end of the island to the other has no sidewalks. There are a couple of one-way streets just wide enough for the bus to fit with about two inches left on each side. In one place, the street is one-way *except for buses*, which means a car halfway through must back out if the bus comes. The bus's two-toned horn beeps gently to warn shoppers and children to get out of the way. The sound careens off the walls.

At the far end of the island is the pretty, small port of Chiaiolella, where there are a couple of cafés and a hotel. The port accommodates leisure craft. From here you can take the *Metro del Mare*, a boat that makes a circle around Ischia; it departs from the stone pier twice a day at 9:30 and 12:00. It is possible to go over on the earlier run and return in the afternoon. From here, walk around a curve around to the right to find the long narrow strip of black sand beach (Spiaggia Ciraccio), not very appealing because of the litter but lined with snack bars and simple restaurants.

From Chiaiolella, you can walk on a pleasant residential street to the long bridge that leads to Vivara, a small crescent-shaped island that was recently established as a sanctuary for birds. The birds may be protected, but the wild rabbits here are not; *coniglio* is a specialty in most local restaurants. Vivara retains the ruins of a little fort built during the rule of the French and the Palace of the Duke of Bovino, from which there is a view across all of Procida.

Procida is deep Catholic country. There are many little shrines to the Virgin in people's gardens, painted enamel pictures of biblical scenes inlaid in concrete walls. Early one morning we passed four women talking in front of a church, one with a broom in her hand. When the bell tolled the hour, they automatically crossed themselves and went on talking.

The old houses and apartments of the walled town at the top of the hill are built right up against the walls of the church. In the morning, televisions blare, women call down to their children in the street and across balconies to each other. An old man peddles vegetables from his donkey. What a voice. And how freely the women call out to each other and gesture. The basis of opera, all of it.

HOW TO GET THERE

There are frequent direct hydrofoils from Naples at the Mole Beverello and also connecting hydrofoils from the islands of Capri, Ischia, Ponza, and Ventotene, as well as Anzio, on the mainland.

WHERE TO STAY

Hotel Ristorante "da Crescenzio" (Marina Chiaiolella, 80079 Isola di Procida [Napoli]; tel. 8967255) is probably the nicest place to stay on the island, with recently furnished rooms on the second and third floors of a lively restaurant overlooking the port. The rooms are nicely appointed, white with yellow accents, tiled floors, and new baths. Rates vary, depending on the season.

Hotel Celeste Residence (Via Rivoli 6, Chiaiolella; tel. 8967488) has twelve apartments accommodating from two to four persons.

Riviera (Chiaiolella, Via G. da Procida; tel. 8967197) is located on a hill on the road to Chiaiolella. The rooms and balconies have beautiful sea views. The management is not exactly eager to please, but the place is quiet. Moderate.

Slightly more expensive is L'Oasi (16 Via Elleri; tel. 8967499). Two *pensiones*, the El Dorado (tel. 8968005) and the Savoia (tel. 8967616), have moderately priced rooms. A brochure with a complete (short) list of hotels is available at the tourist information bureau at the port.

Rooms and apartments can be rented elsewhere. Information can be obtained from the tourist office at Via Roma 15/bis, Marina Grande. Or try contacting Graziella Travel, Via Roma 13, Marina Grande (tel. 8969594).

WHERE TO EAT

Try a meal of rabbit and local wine at La Medusa or another of the restaurants along the port in Procida. Mille Lucciole is a pleasant pizzeria at the very end of the port, beyond where the ferries dock. A dead-end street near a boat yard makes it very quiet, unlike most places on the island.

YUGOSLAVIA

More than a thousand islands lie along the long stretch of Adriatic coast that forms the western edge of Yugoslavia. Some have been inhabited for centuries; others are empty but for a shepherd grazing his flock in summer. Some, like Hvar and Cres, in the north, are on the tour package circuit now, hosting groups of northern Europeans for sun and swimming. Others, like Lastovo and Vis, are just being opened up to international visitors for the first time. Korčula, which has a connection with Britain going back to the Napoleonic wars, has been widely visited by Europeans for generations but still has an empty, unspoiled feeling except at the height of summer. Islands such as Ugljan and Pašman, in the Kornati group, are primarily Yugoslav vacation spots.

Among the many possibilities to explore, we have included six islands on the southern Dalmatian coast: Mljet, Korčula, Lastovo, Vis (with Biševo), Šolta, and Zlarin. A vacation spent in Dubrovnik-Korčula-Lastovo alone would be an ideal combination of natural beauty, clear water and sun, and historical and artistic riches of the cities. Each island by itself would make an inexpensive, friendly getaway with excellent swimming, boating, fishing, and walking. They are all beautiful. You will not want to leave.

Dubrovnik

We highly recommend you begin your exploration of the coast from the idyllic walled city of Dubrovnik. This well-preserved medieval jewel is a charming place to spend a few days, even though it is crowded with tourists. Formerly called Ragusa, it was for hundreds of years an independent city-state and an important naval power in the region. For most of that time it successfully fended off attempts at domination by both the Turks and the Venetians. Take a day or two, at least, to explore the Plaka, the elegantly proportioned strip of pearly stone that is the pedestrian thoroughfare of Stari Grad (Old Town) and to walk the mile around the top of the city wall, with its fantastic views of tile rooftops and the sea.

In the corner building on your right as you enter Dubrovnik's main gate, you will find the Yugoslav Tourist Office, where you can get maps and general information, change money, find out about rooms to let, and buy concert tickets and inexpensive books and postcards. Travel agencies are good places to inquire about island excursions, should you choose not to take the regular ferries. Try Atlas, Pile 1, tel. 27.333; or Kompas, Marsala Tita 14, tel. 23.186; or Yugotours, Lucarica 1, tel. 24.966.

GENERAL TIPS

A visa is required for all U.S. citizens.

Although swimming is excellent, sandy beaches are few and far between. Those in the know bring a folding rubber mat for sunbathing on the rocks and soft plastic shoes (jellies) to protect your feet against sharp rocks and sea urchins.

When we were there, the value of the dinar decreased daily. For this reason, it is obviously wise to change only a little currency at a time. Because prices and money values are constantly fluctuating, we have usually chosen not to quote prices on Yugoslavia's islands. It is sufficient to say that although prices have increased considerably on the Dalmatian coast in the last few years, they are still low by Western standards, especially for rooms and transportation.

HOW TO GET THERE

There is a ferry that calls at the most important islands and ports along the entire coast: Dubrovnik-Korčula-Hvar-Split-Rab-Rijecka. Unfortunately, this does not help much in reaching the smaller islands, each of which has its own connection to a mainland port. Thus, you can only get to Zlarin from Šibenik, to Vis from Split, and so forth, which makes it difficult to visit more than one or two of the islands in a short period.

For those with sailboats, Yugoslavia is a paradise of idyllic remote coves and pretty harbors. For boat rental, inquire at the Marina Dubrovnik, Komolac bb, 50236 Dubrovnik, Mokosica; tel. 050/87.722. Navigational charts are available at the marina bookstore, along with a *Navigational Guide to the Adriatic*, published by Jugoslavenski Leksikografski. The cost for this very useful book is only about $6. At 18:00 Greenwich Mean Time, yachters can tune in to a U.K. Maritime Network report on weather in the Mediterranean region, including Morse code weather reports from Italy and Spain which have been decoded and translated. (Shortwave 14303, call sign G4FTO.)

Both urban and intercity buses are frequent and reliable. There is no train service along the coast. Boat schedules are geared for both tourists and locals in summer; that is, from many islands, there is both an early morning boat and one that leaves later in the day. After September 15, to leave the islands, you must rise with the local residents who are going to do business in the coastal cities.

Because of rampant inflation, the price of ferries may be different from what is printed on the ticket.

There is an extra charge for suitcases on buses. Do not be surprised if it equals the (low) cost of the ticket. The city bus stations have reliable, cheap baggage storage rooms (*garderobas*), which can come in handy if you want to travel light to an island.

WHERE TO STAY

Although we have listed hotels when they were available, we prefer renting a room in someone's home. The Yugoslavs we met this way were extremely hospitable and generous; it is a great way to meet people and get a glimpse of the way they live. Women with rooms to let will approach you as you get off the bus or ferry. They will always quote prices in German marks. Prices for a double ran from 12 to 30 marks (about $6-$15). You can usually arrange breakfast for an extra charge. We never met anyone who wasn't happy to be paid in marks or dollars, as the dinar is so unstable.

Off-season, you may have to go to the tourist bureau to find rooms to let. If it is closed, ask in a café.

Here are two good addresses for rooms to let in Dubrovnik, both in convenient locations just outside the old city: Marijas Sŏš, Ivana Kukuljevića 15, tel. 050/27467; Nedjelka Batinić, Ivana Kukuljevića 4, tel. 050/24361.

WHERE TO EAT

We found the food in restaurants to be of high quality, although somewhat lacking in variety. As elsewhere in the region, fish is priced by the kilo and is very costly. Scampi and calamari are much cheaper and plentiful. Grilled meats are tasty. Prettily arranged mixed salads are usually available, but we hardly ever saw a cooked vegetable. *Palačinke*, a dessert crepe, is usually the only dessert option. Some Yugoslavian wines are superb. Plavac, a heavy red, was our favorite. Kaštelets is a lighter red. On Korčula, try a bottle of pale, yellowy Grk, flavored with a touch of woodruff, alone or with food.

It is hard to get a good cup of coffee or tea in this country. As our friend Elaine says, "Each cup of coffee is terrible in a different way." Your best bet is to order a "big coffee." You will get a small, but not thimble-sized, Turkish coffee, which has more flavor and punch than the watery cappuccinos and espressos they think tourists want.

RECOMMENDED READING

J. A. Cuddon, *The Companion Guide to Yugoslavia*, New York: Prentice-Hall, 1984.
Celia Irving, *Essentially Yugoslavia*, London: Cristopher Helm, 1988.

Rebecca West, *Black Lamb, Grey Falcon*, New York: Viking Press, 1964.

Mljet

It had to happen. We've got a name that starts with three consecutive consonants. You can't cheat and slide a vowel in there, either: it's not *mill-jet* or *mill-yet*, although the *j* is pronounced like a *y*. You must thrust all three consonant sounds forth on your tongue as if you were hurriedly expelling something distasteful from your mouth. Try it, you'll get a few laughs.

Mljet is a long, skinny island lying just north of Dubrovnik parallel to the Pelješac Peninsula. In terms of natural beauty, it is absolutely the loveliest of the many lovely places we saw along the Dalmatian coast. In 1960, the government designated an area covering about one-third of the island a national park, so it is protected and quite carefully maintained.

The jewels of the park are two inland lakes, Malo Jezero and Veliko Jezero. With a channel connecting them to the sea, they are saltwater lakes; the water temperature is a few degrees higher than in the surrounding Adriatic. The lakes are basins of silky turquoise water rimmed by limestone slopes covered with squatty Aleppo pine. An occasional red-tile roof peaks through. You have the illusion you are in the mountains until you experience the bouyant, tropically warm water.

Although day trippers are abundant and overnight tourists increasingly frequent in summer, in glorious early Sep-

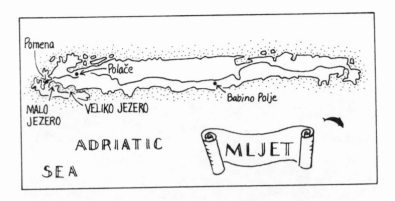

tember we had this lovely island almost to ourselves. We swam off the rocks or strolled the gently terraced stone paths around the lakes, listening to the incessant electronic orchestra of the cicadas. The serene views everywhere we looked evoked the landscapes of Japan.

In the middle of Veliko Jezero, the larger lake, there is a tiny island bearing a lovely monastery that dates from the Middle Ages. Later architectural changes make it look more like an airy Renaissance palace.

Ulysses was supposed to have shipwrecked on Mljet and stayed on for seven years, according to legend, although we also heard this story on Lastovo. In the New Testament Book of Acts, it is told that St. Paul also shipwrecked in the Adriatic, on an island called Melita, which was possibly here or Malta. Roman ruins have been found on the island dating from the second century A.D., when the island was taken over from the Illyrians. There is still a handsome arched wall in the village of Polače which dates from the fourth or fifth century. Later, the island was occupied by Slavs, then given by a Slavic prince to a Benedictine order,

which built the monastery on the lake. Many important persons from Dubrovnik lived here during the time of the Dubrovnik Republic. After the republic fell, the economy declined and the population dropped.

The nearby coastal villages of Polače and Pomena have tourist accommodations. Pomena is within walking distance of Malo Jezero, the smaller, warmer, less frequented lake. From Polače, there is a bus that goes to Veliko Jezero, or you can hike a couple of kilometers through the woods.

For a very peaceful vacation, we suggest spending at least a week on this island, although even a couple of days are worth the trip. If you have time, it would be interesting to explore the parts of the island not included in the park. In the center of the island is the charming medieval village of Babino Polje, and there are several small ports on the northern end which you can see from the ferry on the way to Dubrovnik. There are no tourist accommodations in these places, but you should be able to find rooms to let. Every day during the summer months a green shuttle bus goes from the Hotel Odisseus at Pomena to the far end of the island, where there are good beaches. Off-season, call the hotel for a reservation. They will go if enough people sign up, stopping at Polače along the way.

HOW TO GET THERE

There is a passenger ferry from Dubrovnik (4½ hours) and a car ferry from Trstenik, on the Pelješac Peninsula (1½ hours), both of which dock at Polače. In summer, these run several times a day; off-season, the schedule is drastically cut back. The ferry from Dubrovnik stops at several offshore islands with lovely harbors. It is a very pleasant journey.

Excursion boats making day trips to Mljet from Korčula, Hvar, and Split come in at Pomena. We took an excursion boat one way from Korčula, stayed a couple of days, and took the ferry to Dubrovnik.

WHERE TO STAY

Hotel Melita (Jezero, Govedari 50226, Mljet; tel. 050/32.971), on the tiny island in the lake, was originally the Melita monastery. The setting is splendid, but the rooms were, after all, once monks' cells and retain their ascetic feeling. A room off-season costs $21 per person, $37 for half- board. In July and August, prices go up to $32 for the room, $56 for half-board. Be sure to request a front room, rather than one on the inner courtyard, for the views.

There is no hotel at Polače, but there are several substantial houses with rooms to rent overlooking the sound. From the balconies, you can watch sailboats and the daily car ferry come into the bay. We stayed with Liljana Benkovič, 50226 Govedari, Polače 11.

At Pomena, there is the big, modern Hotel Odisseus, right on the water, as well as rooms to let. (An advantage to staying in Pomena is its proximity to Malo Jezero, the warmer and less busy of the two lakes.)

There is a campground at Polena.

WHERE TO EAT

We were warned by other tourists that food could be a bit of a problem on the island. Shops are not well stocked and restaurants are few. Some of the houses with rooms to let will give you half-board if you request it. You might want to bring fruit and cheese from the mainland.

The Stella Maris, overlooking the bay at Polače, has good grilled meats and a tasty squid and rice appetizer flavored with squid ink. Another, less popular restaurant up the road absorbs the overflow in summer.

The Hotel Melita has a terrace restaurant on the water, a fabulous location with prices to match.

Korčula

"At first sight the richly endowed medieval walled city, small as it is, seems to float on the deep limpid blue sea, completely covering the rocky pinnacle on which it was built for safety, originally with a moat on the landward side. The massive walls and corner towers of the city reflect with a mirror image in the water when the sea is still."

This is how Celia Irving, British author of *Essentially Yugoslavia*, describes the town of Korčula, where she resides.

More than one writer has likened the old city (Stari Grad) of Korčula town to being inside a shattered honeycomb: its compact intricacy and golden light are the same. The main entrance is a bell-shaped stone "flying" staircase, the stones so worn and gleaming they look as if someone had just thrown water on them. The stairs lead up through a covered archway from which the main street, lined with shops and restaurants, slopes upward. At the top of the main road is the Cathedral of Sv. Marco, with carved figures over the main door and a high bell tower. The bishop's palace and a museum can also be found on this irregularly shaped "square." Long, curving passageways, some dotted with shops and cafés, others blessed with residential quiet, drop down to the water on either side. Along these passages you can see many old Venetian houses built with little second-story covered bridges crossing from one side of the street to the other. One of these (follow the signs) is the house where, in 1254, Marco Polo was born. There is a sign in five languages boasting that the famous explorer was a native Korčulan. This is not improbable, as Korčula was a part of the Venetian city-state for seven hundred years. The house has a tiny roofed tower from which there are great views. It is open from May through September from 9:00 a.m. to 6:00 p.m.

Stari Grad has many shops that sell gold jewelry and silver filigree, some set with coral or other semiprecious stones. The silver work is sold by weight, regardless of design. A

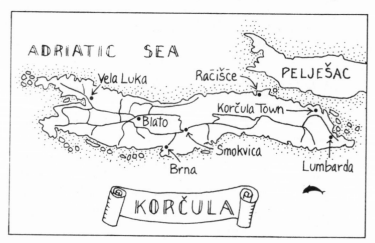

shop called Prodajna iz Losda, the last shop on the right
before you reach the church in old town, sells the delicate
embroidery, crochet, and eyelet work characteristic of this
region. It also displays two magnificently embroidered
antique dresses, one a wedding dress. Several shops also sell
handsome leather belts and handbags. The daily market at
one end of the port also sells embroidery and leather and
rather gaudy multicolored wool rugs. At the base of the steps
leading to the city gate, where vendors have no doubt ped-
dled their wares for centuries, young artisans sell jewelry.
A particularly good buy are pieces made with Russian amber;
the local hematite stones are also pretty. Good artwork from
all over Yugoslavia, reasonably priced, is found at Galeria
Denoble, a little way past Marco Polo's house in Stari Grad.

Do not miss the dramatic Moreška, a traditional sword
dance performed at least once a week during the tourist

season. It can only be performed by people born within Korčula town and is quite spectacular.

The island was probably named by the Greeks after the island of Corfu (*Kerkyra* in Greek). They called it *Korkyra melaina*, dark wood, because it was originally very wooded.

Eight kilometers from Korčula lies the village of Lumbarda, with its fine beaches, where the strong, woodruff-flavored yellow wine called Grk is produced. Fourteen kilometers in the other direction lies the fishing village of Račišče.

If you are staying in Korčula town, take the local bus, which runs 3 or 4 times a day, to Smokvica and walk or hitch from there (4 km) to Brna, a fishing village on a deep bay surrounded by substantial houses. At the west end of the bay there is a mud beach; at the east end, below the Hotel Feral, there are stone walls and platforms where people sunbathe and swim. You can sometimes hire the hotel shuttle bus to take you back up to Smokvica in time to catch the local bus back to Korčula.

The bus from Korčula runs the length of the island, the road dipping and rising over rolling hills covered with cypress and scrub oak, vineyards and old stone houses, in a scene of utter tranquillity. The final destination of this bus is Vela Luka, which means Old Port. This is a quiet town with 5,000 inhabitants and some beachfront hotels. From here you can catch the ferry to the island of Lastovo.

Wandering around the little port town of Vela Luka waiting for the boat to Lastovo, we heard the tight minor chords of a Slavic men's choir. A tape? A mass? We rounded a corner and peered into a courtyard, where twenty or so men in white shirts and blue serge pants, most white-haired but a couple of young ones, were standing in a circle singing. A few glanced over their shoulders at us but quickly turned toward their leader again, leaning forward into the music. With all their souls, their whole beings as one, they sang two exquisite, mournful funeral songs, then broke their circle and headed for the church on the square. As he passed us, their leader noticed I was moved to tears. "Bless God," he said in English, after struggling for a long moment to find the words. I could have cried all afternoon.

HOW TO GET THERE

From Gruž, the boat harbor in Dubrovnik, it is approximately a three-hour ferry trip to Korčula, up a narrow channel between the Sierra-like coastal foothills and a series of low, wooded islands. You can also take a bus to Orebič, on the Pelješac Peninsula; from there, it is a short ferry hop. Atlas and Kompas Tours in Dubrovnik also run excursions to the island.

WHERE TO STAY

Women with rooms to let meet the ferry and quote prices to you in German marks. Twenty-five marks is the standard for a double.

The Hotel Korčula (50260 Korčula; tel. 711-078), built in 1912 and restored in 1982, is a stately old place overlooking the water, with twenty-two double rooms with bath and two singles without bath. A double with breakfast runs about $65. Full board is an additional $45 per person in July and August, but in September and June the rates fall, and in May and October, they are cut to half the summer rates.

WHERE TO EAT

Go up the main street of the old town until you find the sign pointing down the alleyway to the Adio Mare, a crowded, homey spot with seven tables in a stone-walled, open-roofed room overhung with bougainvillea. There are another couple of tables in an enclosed room on the other side of the kitchen. The specialty here is beef. The grilled shish-kebabs are more tender than the stewed meats, but all are tasty. The menu is printed in six languages. Strangers share tables here. It is very popular, so go early. Prices are very reasonable.

To the right, just through the arched entrance to the old town, is the Gradski Podrum, with numerous outdoor tables and several rooms inside. The best bets here are sev-

eral tasty local specialties untranslated on the multilingual menu. They include *duved*, a pork cutlet smothered in a sauce of finely minced vegetables, and *cevapčiči*, minced pork balls served with raw onions and a puree of red peppers. Both are delicious and ridiculously cheap.

Restaurant Liburna, a big modern place with a terrace overlooking the marina, serves the usual grilled meats and salads plus local specialties. Revelin, the pizzeria to the right of the steps to the old city, has a large stone terrace: good pizzas, excellent mixed coffees, and a wild flambéed Irish coffee for which they turn off the lights.

Local wines include Grk, a tangy, high alcohol content white wine flavored with woodruff.

A lively daily market at the foot of the staircase to the old town is a good place to buy fruit and cheese for a picnic. In the supermarket just behind it, you can find bottled drinks, paper goods, and a small selection of meats.

Lastovo

When we were first inquiring about islands to visit in Yugoslavia, we walked into the Yugoslav tourist bureau in Rome and explained our project. The young man at the desk unhesitatingly grabbed our map. "Go here," he said, circling two small islands, Lastovo and Vis. Both have military installations on them, he explained, which meant that until spring 1989 they were closed to international tourists. "Very quiet, very undiscovered." Oh? we thought. Maybe with good reason.

When we told Yugoslavs along the coast that we were going to Lastovo, they shook their heads. "You can't, it's not allowed." On Korčula, people raised their shoulders

eloquently when they heard our destination. "Why go there? There is nothing."

On a bus in Korčula, we talked to a woman from Lastovo who looked surprised we would want to come there. "What do you like best about the island?" we asked her. She paused, as if searching for something to like. "Only clean air, clean water, and . . . lobster," she answered with a little smile. Reason enough, it seemed to us.

You can see from the water that Lastovo is really three separate bodies of land divided by small channels. The largest, Lastovo, is connected to Prežba, which forms the north wall of the large bay at Ubli, so enclosed it feels like a lake. West of Prežba lies another island, Mrcara, with only a few houses on it. The name Korčula means "dark wood," but Lastovo is truly a wooded island, making its larger, better-known neighbor look almost dry and barren. Pine and scrub oak blanket the entire island but for a rim of white stone that borders the water like an edge of lace. The ferry docks at Ubli, where most of the rooms to let are located. Ubli has a small, sleepy square with a church and a café or two. Nearby are the ruins of an old Roman church.

From Ubli it is 10 kilometers to the hill town of Lastovo, where the local bus goes four times a day. It is a beautiful ride through forest, with great views down on numerous bays and inlets. Lastovo is a medieval town built against a hillside in an amphitheatrical form, with stone houses with

red-tiled roofs. At the top of the town is a small main street with a few meager shops, a restaurant, and a café. Farther on, there is a pretty stone church and one or two fine large houses. Old men sit on the church steps of a morning, women shop and chat, the church bells ring. A donkey looks up from munching weeds in an alley at the snap of a camera. A slight breeze comes up from the soundless, road-less, vineyard-filled valley, stirring a few lace curtains. Freshly picked cream- and amber-colored squashes lie in piles on terraces next to jars of briny olives. People are friendly, if a bit surprised to see you. Foreigners are still a phenomenon. When thinking about the town of Lastovo, the word "lost" comes to mind. Lost in time, and secret, lost to the world. This is one of the quietest, most pic-turesque places we have ever seen.

Between Ubli and Lastovo, a road drops down to the tiny settlement at Zaklopatica, a ring of substantial old and new houses around a perfect circle of bay.

On the other side of the island is yet another tiny set-tlement, Scrivena Luka, which does not have electricity as yet but where, again, the houses that ring the bay look quite substantial.

All around the island the water is crystal clear and sparkling, perfect for swimming. The seaward side is made up of sheer white granite cliffs. Here you can see the first lighthouse on the Yugoslav coast, built in the time of Austrian Emperor Franz Josef. If you can find someone to take you out in a boat, or if you are a good walker, there are many splendid coves where you will be entirely alone to swim off the rocks.

Knowledge of the history of the island is spotty. Illyrians, Greeks, and Romans occupied it in ancient times. In 1523, it became a part of the Dubrovnik Republic, unlike nearby Korčula, which was Venetian. Until the nineteenth century, it had a prosperous agriculture and coral industry. The island belonged to Italy from 1918 until the end of World War II; some of the older generation speak Italian.

The military presence on the island is not terribly obtrusive. On the ferry you will see a few young sailors in their brown uniforms with blue and white striped middies, and occasionally an army truck or two will come and turn around in the town plaza. If you take a boat ride around the island, you will see several gun emplacements on the seaward side and bright yellow signs in several languages warning you not to take photographs.

It might be interesting to be in Lastovo at Carnival time (Jan. 6-Ash Wednesday), when various unscripted street dramas are acted out with puppets and the traditional sword dance is performed. On festival days, Lastovans wear traditional red and black costumes trimmed in gold braid. The men wear bowler hats!

The gracious woman in the tourist office in Lastovo town (who speaks German but not English) told us that in

1989, the first time in forty years that Lastovo has been open to tourists, there were 700 foreign tourists (but no Americans) who stayed in private rooms, in addition to those at the Hotel Solitudo. The majority of the visitors so far have been German and Italian.

The vast majority of those 700 tourists were long gone by the time we arrived in *early* September, when the weather was perfect and the welcome very warm. This is a lovely, out-of-the-way spot with clean air, clean water and . . . lobster. According to legend, Calypso detained Odysseus here for seven years. If so, it was not a bad fate.

HOW TO GET THERE

You can take the ferry to Lastovo from Split (5 hours). On the way it stops at Vela Luka, Korčula, so if you happen to be on that island, you can pick it up there (1½ hours). It runs every day all year, arriving in the port of Ubli at 7:30 p.m. and leaving at 4:30 the next morning, except Sunday, when it leaves at a leisurely 9:00 a.m. In July and August, a second run is added to the schedule, with a boat that leaves the island at 2:00 p.m. In our experience, these boats are not yet geared up for the tourist trade. We recommend using a rest room *before* you board.

WHERE TO STAY

We were told at the tourist bureau that there are 600 beds available in private homes; Lastovans are poised and ready for visitors.

At the harbor at Ubli, if you follow the road to your left

marked "Pasadur, 3 km," after a short distance (about 100 m), you will find several large houses that have rooms to let with windows on the sea. Across the street, there are steps down to the water for swimming. We stayed with Tonko and Franka Borovino, who have four large rooms with great views of the water at $7.25 per person ($8.75 with breakfast). If they cook dinner for you, the price per person per day goes up to $18. Both native to Lastovo, they speak fluent Italian and are truly hospitable people. They constantly pressed grapes and homemade wine on us, and it did not take much encouragement to get them to bring out the family photograph albums as well. Out of the goodness of his heart, Mr. Borovino took a handful of his guests for a boat ride around part of the island, where we swam in a crystalline cove. They cannot possibly keep up this level of hospitality once they start getting more tourists. Stay there! (Tonko and Franka Borovina, 50290 Lastovo; tel. 050-80057.)

In Pasadur, there is the Hotel Solitudo, an old establishment that has been refurbished within the last few years. It has 350 beds. The cost per person for a room with breakfast is $15. For $20, you can get full board. The hotel is open from May 1 to October 30 at present, with plans to stay open longer when tourism increases.

The "hotel" in Ubli is used only by the military.

There are two campgrounds on the island, one in Ubli.

WHERE TO EAT

We had our best meal in Yugoslavia in Ubli, at the Lagosta, a restaurant up the road to the left of the church which looked so simple and unappealing that we would have passed right by it had it not been recommended. "Meat or fish?" the waitress asks. We order fish and salad. "No salad, soup." OK. Forty-five minutes later, she emerges apologetically with a platter of tiny fish, "because the big fish isn't ready yet." They are delicately deep-fried and superb. We polish them off. Then comes a heavenly soup, a delicate egg-lemon-chicken broth concoction with a little pasta in it. This is followed by a big, tenderly poached white fish surrounded by steamed potatoes. Splendid.

Tonko and Franka cooked us a lobster, which was cheaper than if we had we ordered it in a restaurant. The price is per kilo, and they are expensive. Order in advance and they will have someone catch you one.

Vis/Biševo

The ferry pointed away from the international bustle of the harbor at Split and headed out into the Adriatic between the long slender offshore islands of Hvar and Brač toward the island of Vis. As we passed three sailboats working the dark blue sea in the opposite direction, we suddenly felt like we were on a cruise.

It was a cruise to a place unknown. Like Lastovo, Vis has been closed to international tourists for many years because of its military installations. As one of the country's westernmost points in the Adriatic, it is Yugoslavia's first line of defense; it was in the mountains here that Tito and his partisans were headquartered for several months during World War II. For a time, it was the only place in the

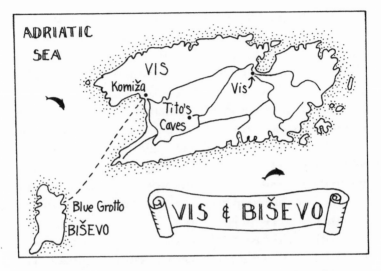

country not occupied by the Axis powers. British commandos arrived in Vis during the war. In fact, the military connection between Vis and Britain goes back to the Napoleonic wars, when the British navy was based here.

The port town of Vis, where the ferry docks, is attractive but has no tourist facilities. We headed for Komiža, the harbor town on the other side of the island, where we knew we could get a boat to the smaller island of Biševo. Its Blue Grotto is one of the main reasons to come to Vis. We crammed into the waiting bus, wishing we had hurried to get a seat. It is no fun to stand up on twisting mountain roads.

Our initial impression of the island was disappointing. The landscape is dry and rocky, with little vegetation. The vineyards are far from lush looking, and many of the intricately terraced fields no longer support any agriculture. Only a few goats scamper here now.

The disappointment does not last long, however. With its view of the valley and the very pretty harbor town of Komiža, the journey down the other side of the mountain is spectacular. The town is of substantial size. The multi-story stone houses have red-tile roofs, and some along the harbor have balconies with a Venetian flavor. Stone streets meander up and down; narrow passageways give onto the sea. There is a broad promenade along the harborfront, where most of the village socializing takes place. At night, when the men sit chatting and smoking in the cafés along the port and the moon beams over the perfect curve of harbor, this is a very romantic spot.

Early on, the island was colonized by the Greeks, who called it Issa, after a girl from Lesbos beloved of Apollo. The Greeks were followed by the Romans. Many of the lovely old stone houses in Vis and Komiža date from medieval

times. Like Lastovo, Vis belonged to the Italians during the two world wars. Italians were apparently looked on with favor, for many of the older islanders are fluent in the language, and you can hear Italian radio stations coming from shops and homes.

Swimming is not wonderful in Komiža, compared with other places we went in Yugoslavia. There is what they call a beach behind the fish factory, but it is rocky and littered with trash. At the far end of the harbor, there is another small beach. It is better to take the boat to Biševo, where the swimming is wonderful.

Komiža has a fishing museum located in the old seaside tower, where different kinds of fishing gear are displayed in an interesting way.

From Vis, you can (must!) take an all-day excursion to the nearby island of Biševo. The boats that go to both the grotto and the beach leave from Komiža at 9:00 a.m. and 12:00 noon and return around 5:00 p.m. This is the summer schedule. Off-season, there will be a morning boat when there are enough people. Another boat that goes only to the beach/settlement leaves at 8:00 a.m. daily. Check times and purchase tickets at the tourist bureau.

The best view in Komiža is from an early morning boat out of the harbor, when you can see the sunlight on the ancient stone buildings. The day we went, the water in the channel between Vis and Biševo looked like finely crinkled paper. Photographers take note.

Biševo is a small, dry, maquis-covered lump with the tiniest settlement on it. "How many people live in Biševo?" we asked. "When we counted them last, there were thirteen." As the excursion boat nears the island and cuts back its engines, a religious quiet descends. To visit the grotto, you transfer onto a waiting rowboat that maneuvers through a cave entrance so low you have to duck and penetrates into a high vaulted cave. Here the light mysteriously

seeps into the water, illuminating the lapis depths. This gorgeous place is one of God's secrets. Go.

Once back in brilliant, ordinary daylight, the excursion boat delivers you to Biševo's sandy (for a change!) beach, where you are free to swim all day in the clear waters of the deep rectangular harbor. Bring a picnic or plan a fish lunch at the local restaurant.

Another interesting excursion is a visit to the caves that were Tito's headquarters during the war, located near the top of Mt. Hum, the island's highest point. If you have a car, follow the coast road from Komiža about 7 kilometers. Along the way, you will have a beautiful view of the water and Komiža from the cliffs. Everywhere there are ancient stone terraces. The piles of stone where the fields have been cleared make you think of old grave mounds; they certainly are monuments to the centuries of hard labor eking out a living from this rocky soil. After 7 kilometers, you will see a sign for Tito's caves pointing up the road to your left. After two more kilometers, you will come to an unmarked stone staircase. A 15-minute climb will bring you to this important historical site. You can also get a cab or a local bus from Komiža to take you there.

Vis had only been open to international tourism a few months when we visited, but German television had already been there to make a film about it. We predict an influx of visitors they scarcely seem to be prepared for. Because it is not terribly easy to get to and lodging and food options are limited, maybe it will stay lost and peaceful for a few more years. Go soon.

HOW TO GET THERE

There is a daily ferry back and forth from Split to Vis, but it does not leave at the same time every day, so check the boat schedule in a tourist office somewhere. Some of the ferries stop at Hvar, so it is possible to get to Vis from that island.

WHERE TO STAY

In Komiža, rooms at the modern Hotel Biševo (Komiža 58485; 058/71.695) go for $25 per night, including breakfast.

No one hustled us for rooms when we got off the boat or bus. Thus, for the first time on the trip, we had to resort to getting a referral from the tourist office. We got clean, *very* simple, *very* cheap rooms over the pizzeria, with an exquisite view of the harbor. The rooms at the far end of the port have less late-night restaurant and café noise. Rooms in "Gusla's house" were recommended by German tourists we met.

In addition to the small hotel at Biševo, someone told us, "You can rent rooms, but only if people know you first." From our $5 room in Komiža, where we shared the spacious family terrace, we could survey the entire harbor and watch the changing light. Our favorite time there was early evening. As the cafés began to fill, the singing from the church at the end of the street blended with the sound of children's voices and the water lapping below.

WHERE TO EAT

Konoba Totac, right on the water at the north end of the bay at Komiža, is very clean and pleasant, with indoor and outdoor tables and a grill. However, when we were there in September, they were out of half the items on the menu, which was expensive, and the service was quite slow. At the other end of the port is a pizzeria and a good fish restaurant called the Riblji, down a few stairs to a spacious and pleasant basement room. Up a narrow street from the harbor is the Bančič, a smoky little place with a television which serves Dalmatian specialties. It was highly recommended but so crowded we never could get in. Several coffee bars complete the options.

There is a restaurant at the hotel at Biševo, but the best bet is the place right next to it, which consists of a few outdoor tables and a barbecue. You choose your fish from the morning's catch in the cool chest, then sip something cold in the sun or take a swim while the fire is stoked up. They strike a gong when the food is ready, usually much later. All the people from our excursion boat ate there; things got very convivial. Do not expect the simplicity to come cheap, though; they have a corner on the market.

Šolta

This island, an hour by boat from Split, is much smaller and less visited than its nearby svelte sisters, Hvar and Brač. It is not in the Yugoslavia guidebooks and does not even publish a map. But "it's a little Hawaii," Šoltans say, "a little California." The weather is gorgeous, and there are carob trees and stubby palms that look like pineapples, plus aquamarine water and lush Mediterranean light. Šolta is fertile enough to support the growth of vineyards and carob trees, whose long dark pods are processed into baby food. The white stone of Šolta is the same as the stone used in building the White House and Sacré-Coeur, which came from the neighboring island of Brač.

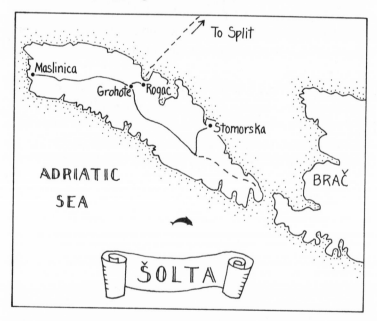

Some Šoltans lament that there isn't big investment capital for hotels, on the cliffs overlooking the exquisite narrow harbor at Stomorska, for example. But there isn't. So there is only the pretty little harbor, two restaurants, and fine swimming.

Rogac, the town where the ferry docks, is nothing special. The peaceful interior village of Grohote is full of old stone houses with low slate roofs. The church in Grohote, Sv. Ivo (St. John), was built by a nineteenth-century Yugoslav who went to Asia and made a fortune, returning home to show his gratitude. On the outskirts of Grohote is an even more peaceful cemetery built around a 300-year-old Benedictine monastery. On the other end of the island from Stomorska is a similar small harbor town, Maslinica. In between is Nečujam, a settlement designed for vacationers, with bungalows, tennis courts, restaurants, and a rocky beach.

We went to Stomorska and relaxed for a few days. There are few enough foreign visitors on Šolta so that anyone who does more than come in overnight on a sailboat gets a little attention. By the second day we were there, we heard people say "American, American" as we approached.

We found Šoltans as interesting as they found us. There is a man who lives on a boat in the Stomorska harbor with his pet, a black sheep who follows him around like a dog, and another who had just returned to his village after living in Argentina for 62 years. A widower no longer able to speak his own language, he stands outside the café speaking Spanish to anyone who will listen.

We were taken in tow by a retired ship's engineer, Joško, who introduced us to Rina, owner of the Komin café and

pension. "Rina will drive you into the hills," he promised, "Rina will show you her village and her farm." Rina, a trim, muscular woman wearing jeans and a T-shirt that says "G'Day" on it, is not eager. Wrench in hand, she is correcting a plumbing problem, something about too much water in one holding tank, not enough in another. While she wrestles with this, Joško shows us the spacious rooms she rents out above her small restaurant. With her savings and government credit, he tells us, she is building a house next door where there will be twenty more rooms and an outdoor terrace restaurant with space for a disco in the summer. "And that's her boat," he says, pointing to a trim little skiff in the harbor.

Rina tears herself from her work and we travel up into the hills in her tiny Renault, Joško translating and elaborating. Rina is 46, has a grown son and a seven-year-old. (There is also a husband, but he seems almost incidental.) Despite being under pressure to be two places at once, she stops the car several times to talk to people: she is clearly a key figure in the village. Tension and energy radiate from her back and shoulders, but she is also very gentle. Children look at her adoringly. At Joško's insistence, we stop to visit the church. She crosses herself and is respectful to the priest; observing some ritual or superstition, she insists on walking all the way around the church instead of doubling back after we visit the cemetery outside.

The farm is three goats, a handful of olive and fig trees, a tiny vineyard, and a large chicken house with chickens crammed three to a cage. As we walk around, Rina proudly flexes her muscles. We don't need a common language for me to understand she's showing me how hard she works. "Not much education, but she's clever," brags Joško as if she were family.

In Grohote, she takes us to the rear of the substantial family home, where she flings open the door of a low stone hut used for storage. "This is where I was born," she says, pointing to a stone seat before a small open fireplace, once clearly the only heat source. A bucket hanging from the ceiling drew water from a nearby well. From this hovel straight out of a Thomas Hardy novel, she leads us past a yard with thirty or forty more chickens in it to another building. First, she unlocks the cover of a 200-year-old square stone vat and ladles out a streamer of green-gold olive oil, pressed from her trees. As she does this, her eyes glitter as if the liquid were gold itself. Then she gestures to the three huge vats and the winepress. "Have you tried the wine of Šolta?" she asks. "They used to send it to Spain to help them color their *riojas*." From a raffia-covered jug that comes up to her knee, she sloshes out a glass, holds it up to show its ruby color. We swig it down. It is wonderful.

HOW TO GET THERE

There are several ferries per day from Split to Rogac, a trip of about 80 minutes. Day excursions also run to Nečujam

from Split. Two buses meet the ferry. One goes to Maslinica and the other to Nečujam and Stomorska.

WHERE TO STAY

At the Komin, on the right-hand side of the harbor at Stomorska, there are rooms with private baths to rent above the restaurant, and there will soon be 20 more units in the house next door. Across the harbor, there are also rooms above the Turanj restaurant, many overlooking the water. The only hotel, the Olint, closes September 15. In summer it's full of vacationing Hungarians, we were told. (Tel. 058/42.228.) At Maslinica, you can stay at the Hotel Avlija, a restored medieval castle. (Tel. 058/654.140.)

WHERE TO EAT

People who come in to Stomorska on their sailboats head for the Turanj, with its inviting terrace on the water. *Turanj* means winepress, and there is an old one in the restaurant, as you would expect. Jašco, the owner's son-in-law and a young father himself, waits tables and will recommend a glass of Kastelets to you, ''wine you can drink like milk.'' It's fun to watch lively Jašco switch back and forth from English to German with the same deftness he must use changing records during his winter job as a disk jockey in Split. Locals and long-term vacationers are more likely to be found at the Komin, with its several tables outside.

Zlarin

*"In season there are too many people. They come and lie
on the rocks and swim, and eat in the one restaurant. But
the season is short, only six weeks, and after that the
island is empty. September has the best weather: you can
still swim in the sea. After that the strong north wind—
the* bora*—begins to blow."*
—Boris Radošević

Zlarin is a small island a short distance from the coastal
city of Šibenik, an hour north of Split. With its old stone
houses, red-tile roofs, and narrow harbor set in a pretty,
protected bay, substantial-looking Zlarin resembles a Dutch
or northern French port. If you arrive, as we did, on the
afternoon boat in mid-September, there is an odd pathos
about it. The shops are shut, the streets are empty, a light
breeze sings through the trees and unkempt grass of the
narrow park that bisects the town. Around six o'clock,
things pick up. Old women dressed in worn black clothing
with red trim—traditional dress on the island—gossip
together on benches, housewives emerge to shop in the
two small grocery stores, a few Germans dock their sailboats and settle into the café for a beer.

Zlarin is known as the coral island. Twenty or so Zlarin-
ers once made their living diving for coral and polishing it
into pretty shapes for jewelry. Only one of the craftsmen,
in his seventies, remains. His attractive little shop on one of
the town's back streets does a thriving business from the
tourist trade. He will proudly show you his trunkful of rough
coral as well as photographs of the island in former days.

The swimming is excellent on the island, the water

kept clear and pure by fast-flowing currents from the north. On the left side of the port, there is a long, concrete wall where you can lie in the sun and swim off the rocks. On the other side of the harbor, past a series of large, rather seedy-looking villas, a path meanders through a small stand of pine trees to a rocky beach.

The long, indented natural harbor provides attractive

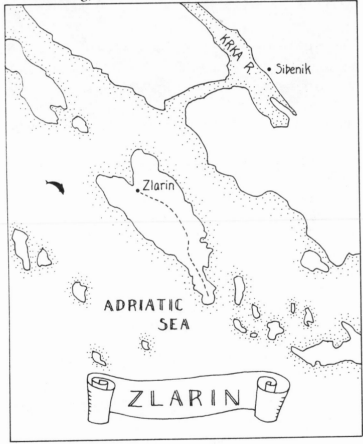

shelter for sailboats. (It had strategic importance for the partisans during the war.)

In summer, there are excursion boats from Zlarin to other islands in the Šibenik archipelago, such as Pršit and Vodiče. Visiting them by regular ferry is tricky, as the ferries are geared to getting people from all the islands to the mainland rather than to visiting between the islands.

Only a half-hour boat ride from Šibenik's pleasant port, Zlarin would be a clean and quiet home base from which to visit that interesting but none-too-clean city. Be sure not to miss the barrel-domed cathedral of Sv. Jakov (St. James), built entirely of stone, with its Gothic porch giving onto a pretty square.

It is also possible to take an excursion boat from the port at Šibenik up the Krka River to the Krka Falls, a series of seventeen lovely natural cascades that are a national park. A path with stone stairs winds up and around them. Do not expect wilderness here. Every 10 meters, you are likely to pass a peasant woman selling figs, cheese, or homemade spirits. There is even a small market selling the ubiquitous rugs and lacework. If you are seeking more solitude, you can hire a smaller boat to take you to nearby lakes. Admission to the park is a steep $5 per person. The round-trip boat ride costs about $9.50 and takes about one and a half hours. You can also get to the falls by car.

Zlarin is in a trough midway between once having an indigenous community with a poor yet viable economy and becoming an escape for tourists and urbanites. The young people have left the island to seek work in Šibenik or Split. Many of those who remain commute the half hour to the city or live in the city and come home weekends. The man who runs the excursion boat *Kristen* goes to New York in the winters to work as a housepainter. There is only one fishing family left on the island.

Such a lovely serene spot, easily accessible from the mainland, is an obvious tourist haven, but because there is no investment capital to develop a tourist infrastructure of restaurants and hotels, it remains a quiet eddy except at the height of summer. The few who have been able to invest money in the tourist business, such as the owner of the restaurant and a few people who have built additions on their houses for tourist rooms, are viewed with some resentment by the wage slaves who have to commute to Šibenik to earn a living. Some of the older residents are resentful of the tourists. The black-garbed old women did not want us to take their picture. We were told they thought we would make fun of them by showing people at home their old worn clothes. Caught in a tuck of time, the future of Zlarin has yet to be imagined.

HOW TO GET THERE

Take the bus (frequent and cheap along the coast) or drive to the port at Šibenik. (There are no cars on the island.) The daily ferry to Zlarin (more frequent in summer) is called the *Ohrid*, which surely must be the Serbo-Croatian term for "old tub." But when we teased our seagoing friend Boris about the thirty-year-old boat, he scoffed at us. "Ha! These old boats hit a rock and keep right on going. It's the new ones, like the *Andrea Doria*, that go right down."

WHERE TO STAY

The reasonably priced Hotel Koralje was virtually empty in September but booms in summer. There are many rooms to let. Apply at the tourist bureau, or if it is closed, ask at the restaurant. We stayed with Boris and Blaga Radošević, Park Skoyevaca 29, 59232 Zlarin; telephone 059/72881.

WHERE TO EAT

The Hotel Koralje has a restaurant, but we never saw anyone eating there. Jurič Iviča, an enterprising Zlariner who spent seven years in Australia, has a corner on the restaurant market, with his Gostionica Ronilac. Jurič's prices are higher than those we encountered on the other islands, but his portions are generous and he has a bit more variety. We ate veal here for the first time in the country, for example. He is a very amiable restaurant host, graciously acting as his own waiter.

GREECE

Some of the smaller, less-frequented Greek islands are so delightful that we developed the Greek Ship Owner's Conspiracy Theory: word must have gone out from some boardroom in Athens or some yacht off Andros that the lure of wild Serifos, the colors of Kastellorizo, *should be kept a secret*. Let swimmers and sunbathers have popular Paros and Mykonos, give the day-trippers showy Santorini and Symi; the quieter, subtler, less brilliant places in the Aegean will be held pristine and untouched for a kabal of insiders to slip away to.

One of the surprising aspects of the Greek islands is that each one is special. Even the islands of the western Cyclades, which are but a few miles apart, are very different from each other in appearance and character. The general history of the region has led to some common characteristics, however.

The story of the Aegean islands is one of independence and conquest, of invasion and defense against invasion, of tough rural and seafaring cultures surviving the opportunistic incursions of just about every major civilization in the area. The long succession of occupations begins with the Minoans from nearby Crete. Later, most of the islands were allied with the city-state of Athens. Then they were part of the Roman Empire. During the Middle Ages, the isolated islands were subject to attacks from the Goths, Saracens, and Slavs. After 1200, they were dominated by Venice until the fall of Constantinople in 1453, after which Turkey and Venice vied for control. There was even a brief annexation of some of the islands by the Russian Empire in the eighteenth century, but it was Turkey that dominated until the Greek revolution of 1821. In the twentieth century, they were frequently used as bases during the major wars.

To protect themselves against invaders by sea, the population enclosed themselves in walled cities, often at the hilliest, least accessible spot on the island. As a result, the islands tend today to have two major settlements, one at the harbor and one in the interior hills.

The hill village, usually called Chora (sometimes spelled Hora), is typically built around a medieval castle (Kastro, sometimes spelled Castro). These are often at or near the highest point on the island, with splendid views. If you look carefully, you will often notice fragments of Doric or Ionian columns built into stone staircases or castle walls. On many islands, the lovely whitewashed houses of the Chora, with their brightly painted doors, are undergoing a careful restoration process. Twisting alleys and steep staircases wind around the interconnecting houses in a way that makes it hard to make a distinction between public and private here. If you wander around, you may find yourself inadvertently staring through someone's open doorway or bumping into a woman hanging out her wash.

The harbor towns are more turned out toward the

world than the sheltered hill towns. Here ferries and fishing boats come and go, and vacationers lie on the beaches or swim off the rocks. Hotels and rooms to let can be found in the harbor where sometimes—as on Serifos and Tilos—there are none to be had in the Chora.

In general, the hill towns are where the islanders retain their sense of community. If pirates once attacked from the sea, now vacationers invade the shores: the retreat to the hills is the same. The result? The Chora can be a more authentic place to get a taste of Greek village culture and experience its traditional hospitality. You may prefer to be near the water, however, and it is easier to negotiate the sometimes erratic boat schedules if you are 10 minutes, or 5, from the dock. Whatever your choice, there is always bus transportation to the Chora from the harbor which is coordinated with the boat schedule.

The major mark of the Byzantine civilization that survived the countless invasions are the Greek Orthodox monasteries that crown most of the islands. Usually deserted now, they are still maintained and often opened for an annual procession and liturgy. In addition, the islands are dotted with tiny white chapels, often with bright blue roofs. They make a wonderfully bright visual counterpoint to the soft browns and greens of the surrounding stone-terraced landscape. These are usually locked, as they belong to individual Greek families.

Some would say that none of the invasions of foreign armies in the Aegean has had such a profound effect as the influx of tourists in the last twenty years; others shrug off the onslaught of tourism, saying that after centuries of marauders, the islands can survive anything. None of the islands we visited is dominated by tourism, but all have their share of summer visitors determined to find their beauty and sunshine off the beaten path. In varying degrees, the local economies have come to depend on tourists; some of the islands would be almost totally depopulated but for the income from rentals and restaurants.

Again and again, we encountered other visitors who wanted to shut us up. "You're not going to write very much about this place, are you? Say it's terrible, windy, deserted, the people unfriendly. We don't want a lot of tourists here." But these were travelers who had discovered the place for themselves or native islanders who had returned here after a long stint in Athens or abroad. We were reminded of the restaurant reviewer, who, implored by his friends not to tell about their favorite finds, finally went to the restaurant owners themselves. "Do you want me to write about this place or keep it a secret?" he asked. "My friends are afraid I will spoil it." Of course, they got down on their knees and begged him to write.

WHERE TO STAY

As in Yugoslavia, local inhabitants with rooms to rent meet the boats and buses. However, after October 1, the locals may not be expecting tourists, which means you may have to walk into town and look around. Prices are considerably lower off-season, and you can usually strike a bargain that is a bit lower than the asking price, although the prices are so reasonable that it hardly seems worth the trouble, or even fair, to do so. In October 1989, the lowest we paid was

850 drachmas ($5) for a single on Tilos; the highest, 2,400 drachmas ($15) for a double with private bath on Serifos. Both were simple and clean, in excellent locations. Be sure and ask about hot water. Solar hot water systems are common, which means that the hot water supply is most reliable between 10:00 a.m. and 4:00 p.m.

WHERE TO EAT

In the Greek islands, the generic restaurant is called a *taverna*, where you have a choice of two or three prepared dishes: moussaka or stuffed tomatoes or roast chicken, for example. You can go in the kitchen and have a look. (Greeks do it, too.) Sometimes there are grilled meats or calamari as well, and usually the lovely garlic and yogurt appetizer called tsatziki. The mixed salad with tomatoes, olives, and feta is almost always available. Local wine is often retsina, flavored with pine resin, but there are sometimes alternatives.

Anything called a restaurant (rather than a taverna) is apt to be more expensive and may not be better. The *kafenions* are frequented mostly by Greek men drinking coffee or ouzo, but they are by no means off-limits to tourists. Nescafe is almost always an alternative to the tiny cups of sweetened Greek coffee.

GREEK FERRYBOATS

On the tiny Greek island of Nissyros, in the eastern Aegean, the owner of a local taverna blinks his lights on and off every time the ferryboat *Kalymnos* passes by, and from the ferry, the lights dim and brighten in response. The boat captain and the restaurant owner went to school together but have not seen each other since. "How does he look?" the restaurant man asked a frequent passenger who was having a meal at his place. "Does he look the same as when we were in school?"

Ferryboats are the lifeline of the Aegean islands, which have only a handful of airports among them. As the donkey is the beast of burden high in the stony mountains where there are no roads, so the ferry serves the water routes, hauling goods and passengers.

All the commerce and energy of the islands focus on the docking of the ferry. The smaller and sleepier the island, the more intense the vortex of activity surrounding the loading and unloading of the big boats. The ferry looms into sight, monstrously big and white. At night it twinkles on the horizon out of nowhere, then grows into a shining vision of a giant city pressing in out of the darkness. It bears down on the concrete quay, then swings around so it can dock rump first. As it turns, it is already lowering the huge back flap. Lines fly from the stern corners to the quay. Three-inch hawsers are flung ashore and looped over huge iron posts, then winched tight while, high on the stern, an officer barks harsh commands. Out of the huge black hole above the stern gate, the ferry expels, pell-mell, old Greek women in black covered with packages, German backpackers, Greek businessmen with their suitcases, French teenagers, huge Mercedes trucks, diesel fumes, pale British sun seekers, Dutch hippies, Scandinavians with bicycles, pickup trucks full of vegetables or furniture.

The huge low blast of the ferry whistle generates an

equal amount of activity and excitement on shore. Big
diesel trucks belch their way on board and feisty little cars
jockey their way backward into position. Tourists and
Greeks elbow their way up the ramp past the crewman
checking tickets and charge up the narrow stairways that
flank the hold of the ship, bumping into passengers still trying to disembark. Crew members roll goods in and out of
the hold in wheelbarrows, shouting at each other and ges-
ticulating with their heads. A postal employee exchanges
one green sack marked *postes helleniques*, usually only half
full, for another. On shore, a dozen men and women
hustling *dhomatia*, rooms to let, *Zimmer*, mill around the
fresh delivery of tourists.

On the islands that export fish to Athens, such as Symi
and Kimolos, high-booted fishermen in slick blue or
orange aprons, cigarette at the lip, form a line to load their
day's catch. The men each seize by their corners two
wooden crates of silvery fish, forming a daisy chain of men
and crates to load the fish onto the boat. In this age-old
cooperative dance, the men re-form the chain again and
again until all that remains of the stack of boxes are a few
mackerel that have slithered from the pile, to be clawed
over at once by the harbor cats.

As soon as the last man steps lightly off the boat—or
before—the heavy, rope-coiled pads that make a doormat-
like buffer between the concrete quay and the ferry ramp
are snatched away, and the ramp rises slowly, with a sure-
footed sailor balancing on it as he shouts some last message
to shore. The propeller churns the water frosty blue and
white, the big looped hawsers are eased from the posts and
flop for a moment in the water before they are drawn into

the boat, girlfriends and grandmothers wave once more and shout, *"Khalo taxi!"* (Good trip), before they turn away. Usually, all this takes place within five or ten minutes, reminding us that *chaos* is originally a Greek word.

Dockings can be hair-raising. Once when we came into the port at Milos, a howling west wind swept our ferry away from the pier as it tried to dock. Five times it circled in the miserable crosswind, the huge, high sides of the ferry acting like a sail. Once, the crew got two heavy hawsers around the iron posts of the concrete quay, and the ferry kept right on moving, left to right, as though someone had tied clothesline to a locomotive. On the fifth try, at real risk to both crew and bystanders, the ship managed a brief, wobbly docking. The massive hawsers were stretched hard as iron bars. One was badly frayed; in fear and fascination we watched for it to part.

The island Greeks get dressed up in their city clothes to ride the ferry. Usually Athens-bound, they board carrying well-worn suitcases and bulky packages and head straight for the lounges inside, where they stake out a seat or two they can stretch out on. They seldom travel alone; if not family members, there are always others from their village making the same journey. The men crowd around the bar or share a table, smoking, drinking thimblefuls of gritty black coffee in plastic cups so slick and creamy to the touch it is surprising they do not melt right into the hot, sweet liquid. And talking, always talking, loudly, with gestures, with assurance, so fiercely they sound as if they must be arguing. The women also talk, loudly, or sleep or do handwork. The men outnumber women five to one.

On deck the tourists stake out their slatted wooden

benches in the sun and slough off their tall backpacks. Out come liters of mineral water, beer, retsina, fruit and cheese, a dog-eared novel traded for another on the last island. On one trip we saw a barefoot, boisterous family of gypsies, several bird cages in tow, spread their tattered sleeping bags on deck for a long siege.

Everything comes to a standstill when a storm comes up in the Aegean. If the word goes out from Piraeus that no boat will move on the waters, island-bound tourists undo their packs and retreat into the cafés, and island residents phone their relatives in Athens to put their plans on hold. Should the storm last two or three days, the choices in the tavernas may shrink and fruit disappear from the tiny markets.

The indispensable ferries are scheduled with a broad hand. Every week, a printed schedule of the names and departure times of all boats leaving Piraeus is available from the Greek Tourist Office in Athens. A similar schedule is available in Rhodes for boats leaving that island. Arrive at the dock, however, and you may find that a different boat is going to your destination two hours later. Harbor cafés do a lot of business from people sitting with suitcases scanning the horizon for a boat that was due in at 6:00 and hasn't yet arrived at 8:00. At the other extreme, on Milos, we watched a boat that was not due until midnight dock and depart at 11:00 p.m., rearranging the plans of a number of stranded tourists.

Piraeus and Rhodes may be sure of what boats are leaving from their docks, but they have no idea what the schedules are for the other islands. You can try and piece an itinerary together by deduction from the weekly schedule, or you can assume that even the most remote islands have ferries coming and going a minimum of three times a week in good weather. Since it is foolish to spend less than three days in one of these places anyway, there will be time enough when you get there to find out when the next boat leaves. Just do not rely on a boat schedule to get you somewhere a day before your flight out of Athens.

Getting reliable information is also complicated by the fact that there are different ferryboat companies. On islands big enough to have more than one travel agency, the agency for one company will refuse to give out information about the schedules of another. A better bet is the port police, who are sure to have impartial information the morning of your departure.

After you study the Piraeus schedule for a while, you begin to see a pattern in the way the boats move. There are boats that run down the western Cyclades, Kea-Kithnos-Serifos-Sifnos-Milos-Kimolos. Some of these continue on to Folegandros-Sikinos-Santorini. Another line is down the middle of the Cyclades, Syros-Paros-Naxos-Ios. Some of these also continue to Folegandros, and so on. Frequently a boat out of Piraeus will do a run in the Cyclades and continue on to Rhodes via Crete or Amorgos, Astypalea, and the islands of the Dodecanese. There are express boats from Piraeus to Crete and back and forth from Athens to Rhodes. The summer schedule is dense with possibilities; off-season options are sparser. You may have to return to Piraeus to get to an island you can see from the one you are on.

For people accustomed to freeway and air travel, these boats are slow and the distances small. A square drawn on the map around the Cyclades, for example, shows about

100 square miles on a side, and their midpoint, Paros, is around 100 miles from Athens. Yet a trip to Paros can take 6 to 7 sweet or tedious hours. The pace of the ferry prepares you for the pace of the islands. Let the slow empty hours, the sun and wind, the gentle pulsing of the engines, lull you into sleep or reverie. "*Ciga, ciga*," the Greeks say. What's the rush?

RECOMMENDED READING

Durrell, Lawrence, *The Greek Islands*. London: Penguin Books, 1980. Although Durrell can be dismissive of the minor islands, his love affair with the region is contagious, and he writes like an angel.

Dumont Guide, *Greek Islands*. New York: Stewart, Tabor, and Chang, 1985. Good for specifics on art, architecture, and history of each island.

Cyclades

Folegandros

We took the *Apollon Express* down through the western Cyclades to Folegandros, arriving after dark. With a handful of tourists, we scrambled into the mini-bus waiting at the port and were hauled up a narrow strip of concrete road and spewed out into the main town. Where are we? A stage set for a Cycladic village? Bright electric bulbs are strung across the central square, people are dining at little wooden tables around a circle outlined on the pavement. At stage left, an old man with snowy white hair and stupendous mustaches turns souvlaki on an open grill. At stage right, a dignified young man with black mustaches steps out of a doorway to offer us a room to rent. The bit players are all in place. Old men drink at the kafenion, children run into the small grocery to do a bit of last-minute shopping for dinner. The whole scene is snugly framed by whitewashed buildings and churches. What is this enchanting place?

We took the room, ate the souvlaki, and the next morning set out to discover where we were. We so loved the natural beauty and healthy community life that we considered entitling this book *Folegandros and Other Mediterranean Islands.*

THE COMMUNITY

In his book on the Greek islands, Lawrence Durrell names four communal points that "serve as electrodes...for news, opinion, argument—the factors on which the intellectual life of a village reposes." These are the threshing floor, which is often used as a platform for speech days and

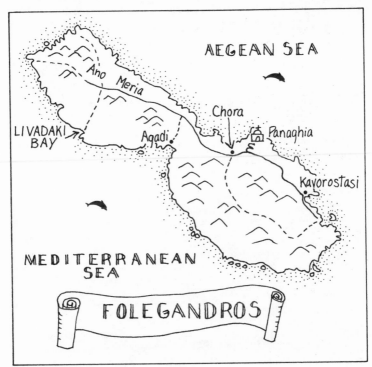

festivals, the village spring, the café, and the communal bakery. On Folegandros, all four of these meeting places are to be found in or near the central square. The large painted circle in front of the church is indeed an old threshing floor. The village taps, turned on a few hours a day so people can come and fill their containers with water, are here. The major tavernas and the kafenion are all within sight of each other, and you can sit in any one of them and watch people carry their prepared dough across the square to the bakery, where, for a small fee, they do their baking after the baker has finished hers. People from the countryside trot in on their donkeys, old men gather to sit in the sun and gossip, a taverna owner, varnishing chairs, may be assisted by several children.

The ongoing vigorous exchange of information and drama in the village square says much about the character of the island. Of all the islands we visited in the Mediterra-

nean, it seems to have the healthiest community life. Unlike islands where the only remaining indigenous population is elderly, the population of Folegandros is increasing. In

a population of 650, there are over 100 young people and children. Eleven babies were born on the island last year, a whole new class for the school, as someone pointed out. A high school was built recently, which also helps to stabilize the population, as families no longer have to move with their teenagers to a place where they can continue their education. Unlike many places that have abandoned agriculture for the more lucrative fields of tourism, Folegandros continues to grow vegetables, wheat, and legumes for its own consumption and even exports 1,500 lambs to the rest of Greece at Easter.

Both towns have powerful municipal councils that regulate community life and ensure that it is not dominated by an influx of foreign tourists and money. Local and national regulations place severe restrictions on architectural style and limit the height of buildings to two stories. Even the color of window trim—blue, green, and brown—is legislated, although not everyone respects the law in this matter. Unlike other places we visited whose economic life is dominated by tourism, tavernas are open and buses run a full schedule all year.

Folegandros has one policeman. "What does he do all day?" we ask. "Well, let's see, what *does* he do? There's no crime here. Oh, he mainly monitors prices in the markets." (Under the socialist government of Greece, prices are regulated.)

As is the case with many of the smaller islands that have not played an important role in history, there is no written history of Folegandros. What is known has been pieced together from archaeological findings, letters and documents, and knowledge about the Cyclades in general. In the "Golden Cave," now accessible only by sea and a difficult climb, bones and hieroglyphs have been dated at 3000 B.C. An old Roman water basin was also found here. At the top of the peak where the Panayia monastery is now,

a preclassical altar was found, dating from about 1200 B.C. This was later the site of a temple to the goddess Artemis, which was in turn destroyed when the monastery was constructed in the Christian era. Material from the temple of the rival religion was used to build the church. The monastery as it stands today dates from about 1100. According to church documents in Athens, there was also a convent on the island until 1700, but no one knows where it was located. In earlier times, the residents of the island lived at the top of the hill surrounding the temple so they would be in full view of the gods. In the Middle Ages, in defense against the pirate invaders, they built a narrow enclosed walled city on the cliff. From a distance, the stone walls of the houses blended with the stony cliffs, camouflaging them. Like so many other islands in the area, the island was occupied for a long time by the Venetians, and again by the Turks.

In the absence of written history, the past is surmised and deduced. Spanish gold coins were found recently during the restoration of an old house, giving rise to speculation that at one time the community was actually taken over by pirates. In another house, we saw a ceiling beam that was said to be the mast from a captured pirate ship.

Life in Folegandros has only recently been touched by modernization. The long concrete road that runs up from the port through the two towns was poured only in 1973. The main town was electrified in 1976, the remote village of Epano Meria in 1984; one or two smaller settlements are still without electricity. Running water in private houses is also recent.

As on all the islands, the issue of water is critical. While we were on Folegandros, we experienced a fierce storm in the Aegean. The wind howled down the alleys of Folegandros town and the rain came down in sheets. But this is rare. Water caught in cisterns and wells serves the community for about four months out of the year. The rest of the time water is brought in by boat from Santorini and trucked up the mountain, where it is stored in cisterns. People come and fill their containers at the community taps, which are turned on a couple of times a day. The only named street on the island is the one that slopes down beside the old square. It's called the "Danube" because when it rains, water rushes down it and is caught in a cistern at the bottom. New homes have running water, and owners of older homes can now buy into the system, but many have not.

In one of the village squares, you can still see wells, a place for washing clothes, and a drinking trough for animals. Village life used to center around these essential spots. Nearby is the town's main church; the town hall and library are in the building opposite. Here are locust, pepper, and acacia trees for shade: imagine the color when they all bloom at once in the spring!

Folegandros is the one place we visited that we hesitated to include in this book. It seems so healthy, so unaware of being "quaint" or "picturesque." Too many tourists with their cameras and demands will surely change all that. Anna and Fotis Papadopoulos run the Cycladic School, which offers course in painted, drawing, photography, and other arts, as well as sailing and yoga, bringing an influx of northern Europeans to the island for short periods. Anna, who is a Danish sociologist with a passionate enthusiasm for the island, feels that Folegandrans benefit from the exchange with outsiders. "They bring the world in, as well as taking from the place. That way, everybody changes. It's ridiculous to think this place is going to remain static, even to wish for it." Nevertheless, she and others feel that too many tourists might upset the social and economic equilibrium the island now maintains. If you go to this place so magical in its simplicity and natural beauty, please go quietly, with your eyes open, and with respect.

WALKING AROUND

First, we returned to the main square of Folegandros town and, after a leisurely breakfast on the sunny terrace of a taverna, ducked through a nearby archway to enter the old walled city at the village core. The outer wall—the back wall of a row of houses—virtually extends upward from the long, sheer cliff, the stone rampart camouflaged by the dun-colored natural rock. Inside the medieval walls are two or three streets of cramped buildings, now gradually being restored, some with ancient (now plumbed) outhouses perched on their balconies.

Over the centuries, the village has gradually expanded outside the Kastro walls. Several nearby adjacent squares outside the walled town are now the hub of village life; they, in turn, are surrounded by a ring of recently built houses and pensions. Above the town, we could see a path lined with whitewashed stones which zigzags up to the splendid white monastery of Panayia, isolated on the highest slope of mountain. Higher still, at the very peak, is the unmarked site of an ancient temple to Artemis.

The tight, sheltering concentric circles of the Chora contrast sharply with the barren, windswept, open landscape of the rest of the island. The road beyond the village to the upper end of the island runs through beautiful, spare country with splendid views back on the clifftop town and across the water to the islands opposite. On a clear day, you can see Kimolos, Sifnos, and Crete. Along the cliffs about halfway up the road are three imposing windmills. From here there is a magnificent view back on the precariously perched village and the path to the monastery.

Folegandros is made of marble and slate. Much of the marble has a pink cast and the slate is green, the colors of the beautiful, roughly laid walls that terrace and circumscribe the fields everywhere you look. These colors also reflect in the sea, making astonishing combinations. After a rain washes green shale into the sea, gigantic jade-stained scallops of water surround the island, the green color bleeding into the intense blue.

A 4-kilometer climb to the far end of the island's one paved road will bring you to Epano Meria, a village that has no identifiable center. The houses, farms, and chapels stretch out along the narrow road rather like clothes on a line. This

is a walker's paradise, with views of the sea in all directions and an abundance of mule paths wending through the densely terraced fields. Oxen still work the fields here, and donkeys haul dung to the fields and crops out of them. (Trying to take photographs, we were hustled for money once.) The stone circles in the fields are threshing floors, some still in use, and we passed a working blacksmith's shop.

Wandering around here where few tourists come, we had the feeling of being in someone's backyard. Although our "Kalimera!" was usually returned gravely and respectfully, we sometimes also got (did we imagine it?) looks of wariness or puzzlement.

Halfway between Folegandros town and Epano Meria lies an unmarked path leading down to the pretty cove at Agadi. Look for a little concrete bus shelter at the top of the path. If you take the bus, ask the driver to drop you off at Agadi. The beach is gorgeous here, but there are too many rocks for good swimming. For better swimming, you can follow the trails from Epano Meria to Livadaki Bay, which has a dark gray pebble beach surrounded by a wall of light gray polished marble.

The port town, Karovostasi, is essentially a summer establishment; in the winter, there are only five residents. There are a few fishing boats and a pretty pebble beach with clear water. The light is special in the harbor on a sunny day; many painters come to capture the turquoise green crystal water and the purple cast over the land.

Follow the road west of the port to reach the campground, where there is another beach.

HOW TO GET THERE

Ferries leave daily from Piraeus in summer and two or three times a week during off-season. In summer, there are also connections with Paros, Naxos, and other islands in the region.

"How do we find out if the boat is coming?" we asked on Folegandros during a storm. "Well, usually you would ask the travel agent, but she's away for a few days in Athens. Her husband is the postman, however, so he might know.

He has to pick up the mail off the boat. The bus driver usually knows, because he has to know when to meet the boat, but a storm washed out the road from 'Ano Meria, so the bus can't even get down from there. The policeman is supposed to know, but he's new, so he doesn't know *anything* yet." "So, is the boat coming?" "No boats left from Piraeus today. In the morning, we'll see."

WHERE TO STAY

The Hotel Fanis Vevis, located on the upper edge of town, is a dignified old square house with front rooms looking out over the water and side rooms looking over the fields and town. This is a lovely, relaxed old place with a warm and generous owner. A double room is 3,250 drachmas high season, 2,600 drachmas off-season. The hotel also rents a few old farmhouses in the surrounding area which have been refurbished in the original style.

The Hotel Danassi is an ancient building in the old Kastro, right on the edge of the cliff. The view from the cliffside rooms is extraordinary. These are rooms from the Middle Ages!

The Hotel Odysseus, newly established on the edge of town, has rooms with balconies but no private baths for 2,000 drachmas per night during off-season. Around the Odysseus are several houses built specifically with rooms to rent. We found a modern apartment two streets back from the main square for 2,500 drachmas off-season. Ask for Louis at Kritikos' taverna.

There are also rooms to let at the port, if you prefer being near the water.

Although not "discovered" in any sense, Folegandros is crowded with visitors in summer, most of them Greeks on vacation and some of them Europeans looking for an out-of-the-way island. August 15, St. Mary's Day, when people from the island return home, is the busiest time. You will have trouble finding a room then.

WHERE TO EAT

The social center of town, summer and winter, is the taverna with the raised terrace on the main square. It serves breakfast all morning and the basic Greek menu at dinner. Try the *pastitsio*, noodles topped with a layer of meat and a cream sauce, or the stuffed tomatoes. One of the women who works here is said to be one of the finest folksingers in Greece. Next door, Kritikos of the white mustaches serves good grilled meats. Nearby is a kafenion, frequented mostly by Greek men, that also has a breakfast menu in English. A few other tavernas are open only through September. There is a pizza/coffee/ice cream place (its official name is the Rainbow, but it's known as the pizzeria) with a terrace that is a fabulous place to view sunsets. (We were told that when this was built, the women in town felt they had someplace to go when their friends came from Athens. Greek women are seldom seen in the kafenions, which are sometimes called the Greek man's living room.)

At the port, there is a taverna in summer, as well as Evangilo's Bar, which serves a good coffee and ice cream concoction. Hang out here while you wait for the ferry.

There are two tavernas at the beach at Agadi. The first is reputed to serve good food and lukewarm drinks; at the second, the food is lousy, but the drinks are cold.

At Epano Meria, the bus parks right next to a simple taverna with good food.

PRACTICAL INFORMATION

In the Kastro, there is a travel agent who sells boat tickets and exchanges money (there is no bank on the island).

For a brochure about the Cycladic School, write Anna and Fotis Papadopoulos, Folegandros 840-11.

Serifos

Serifos is a small, rocky island lying between Kithnos and Sifnos and not far from Folegandros. "Iron-stained Serifos speaks of poverty and silence," intones Durrell. The harbor at Livadia is "the place. . . to suit novelists and other suicides." "The perfect setting for a horror movie," snarls the Harvard guide. However, on one of the ferries, a vigorous British hiker who has made numerous trips in the Aegean told us it was his favorite island. Curious, we decided to see for ourselves.

We arrived about 8:30 p.m. and were struck dumb by the view from the harbor of the brilliant star-scattering of lights from the Chora, a fairy tale city on the steep hill above. Oh, take us there! Cars, trucks, and motorcycles went shooting past us up a curved road. But we were doomed to stay below at Livadia, the harbor town, for there are no accommodations for tourists in the upper regions. We had the good luck to find a room with a bal-

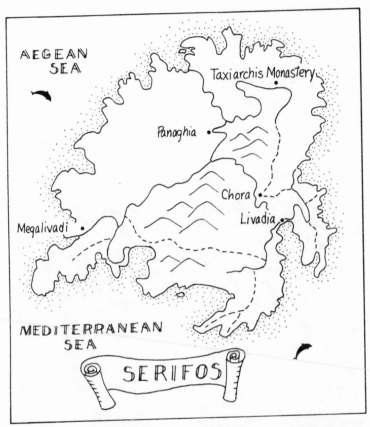

cony looking over the harbor and up at the sparkling dream city.

In the morning, we awoke to look out over a perfect curve of harbor surrounded by hills that seemed almost black in the early morning shadows. At the top of the hill, the white buildings tumbling down the side of the mountain gleamed in sunlight. In daylight, the town still seems to have toppled off the pages of a child's book. Poverty?

Silence? First and foremost, visual splendor!

From Livadia, we climbed a serpentine road five kilometers up the mountain to the Chora, cutting off the curves on the steep stone pathway for people and donkeys. Pausing for breath, we looked out over the protected harbor, with the island of Sifnos in the distance, and up to the shifting angles of the town. At one bend in the road, we peered down into a lovely shaded valley of stone-walled fields, olive trees, and threshing floors, the muted halftones contrasted with the stunning white of a domed chapel.

In the town, most of the houses stand empty but not abandoned: they are freshly painted and whitewashed. Steep, whitewashed stone stairs climb every which way. In October, it was eerily quiet; once or twice, we stumbled on a couple of old women emerging from a dark hole of a shop or, rounding a curve, bumped into a housewife hanging her laundry, or an old man driving a laden donkey through the streets.

The hill town—called both Hora and Serifos on the signs—extends from about halfway up the hill to the very top. At the summit is the old walled city, the Kastro. It is a long climb on narrow stone walkways to the simple white church at the peak; and every step seemed to bring us face-to-face with a new visual feast: crumbling old wooden doors, a bright lavender window frame, geraniums in olive oil cans painted bright blue, an orange cat sunning itself on a step, all seen against a background of brilliant white, in clear, wind-washed air, and in the distance, lovely views of the island and surrounding sea. The view down on the Chora itself—with blue, red, and green painted doors on many cubicle houses and one handsome red-domed church—is especially striking. If you squint, all is a blur of color and geometric shapes. This must have been the original inspiration for cubism! The spray-painted slogan "Punk's not dead!" on a nearby wall hardly dented the sheer, timeless, sun-seared splendor of the place.

Below the Kastro, there are two town squares, the upper one, formal and deserted, contains a substantial church, Aghios Athanassious, next to a city hall with a handsome, neoclassical facade. Still lower on the hillside is a rundown square, the real village center, sporting two or three extremely simple tavernas and a joint called Stavros café bar, which has a stunning view. We ate at the blue-trimmed "kafe," the only one with a sign, because it looked the most welcoming. The friendly woman who runs it offered us a choice of pork chops or *ravissia*, a bowl of melt-in-your-mouth garbanzo beans cooked with onions and olive oil and served with the best bread in Greece. After the climb up the mountain and a couple of hours in the sun and wind savoring the magical views, it was a heavenly meal. We were the only non-Greeks around; the rest of the customers were unshaven old men with caps on, sitting behind their little white cups of dense coffee and ritual glasses of sediment-chasing water, smoking and looking us over.

After the iron mines that were the major economic base on the island were closed, Serifos' Chora was virtually a deserted city, but now it is being repopulated by foreigners and Athenians who are buying and renovating houses. The island is close enough to the mainland so that Athenians can come here on weekends. Many foreign artists and architects have homes in the Chora, where they have carefully preserved the old look of the place. When Melina Mercouri was Greek minister of culture, she designated the

Chora on Serifos as one of the most beautiful towns in Greece.

In addition to the glorious hill town, the island has other sights and pleasures. In summer, the splendid sheltered harbor at Livadia is busy with sailboats coming in and out and swimmers on the beach. Next to the harbor, immediately over the hill from the concrete quay, is another shapely cove with a sand beach. Looking over it is the outdoor bar called Relax. Continue to walk along the coast for other beaches.

Legend has it that Perseus and Danae, set adrift on a boat, were washed ashore on Serifos. After a series of intrigues in which Polydeuces, one of the Serifos kings, tried to force Danae to marry him, Perseus, her son, turned the king and his cohorts into stone by forcing them to look at Medusa's head. The stones are the stony mountains of the island. We understood this legend better after we traveled the hardscrabble terrain to the far end of Serifos.

We went, mostly on foot, the 16 kilometers from Livadia to visit the Taxiarchis monastery, in a lonely hillside setting looking out at the water. We were told there was one monk left who would let us in for a look, but no one answered our calls and knocks, and we only got a peek through a crack in the tiny wooden door at the lovely inner courtyard. (It is best to phone ahead for an appointment, we were later told.) We communed with a few chickens scratching near the roadside and investigated the twin chapels and tiny cemetery across the street. Inside one of the chapels were shelves of boxes labeled with names and photographs. It is the custom in rural Greece to unbury the dead after three years and box up the remains.

Walking the long, empty road back (on a Sunday afternoon there were no buses running or cars moving), we stopped at Panaghia to have a peek at the island's oldest church, a tiny Byzantine chapel dating from the tenth century. It is at the center of a warren of houses in the dreary little village about halfway between the Chora and the Taxiarchis monastery. The coastal village of Megalivadi is said to be the site of the first workers' strike in Greece. The iron miners were being paid one drachma a day to work from dawn until dusk. When policemen were sent in by the Greek government to break the strike, the wife of one of the miners pushed a policeman into the sea. All in all, ten people were killed, five workers and five policemen. The way the old islanders tell it, the road all the way from Megalivadi to Hora was stained with the blood of injured workers. The strike was successful; the workers' demands were met. From then on, they got paid two drachmas for an eight-hour day.

"Go to Megalivadi," we were told, "it's lovely." On this pretty harbor, houses were built in a neoclassical style for the bosses of the iron mines. Now they stand empty, a ghost town. "Like a Mexican town," someone said. But it's a two-to three-hour walk one way over a road so bad that taxis are reluctant to go and will charge 3,000 drachmas. In calm weather, it is possible to hire a boat to take you there. We confess we did not make it, so we have an excuse to go back to one of our favorite islands.

HOW TO GET THERE

The *Kimolo*, cleanest ferry in the Aegean, goes along the western Cyclades from Piraeus. There are boats two or three times a week, more frequently in summer. The charge is 1,300 drachmas.

WHERE TO STAY

Livadia is lined with hotels named the Perseus, Kyclades, and the like, all modern, utilitarian places. The one with the best view is the Hotel Anefi, on the hill directly above the concrete quay where the ferry docks. The cost is 4,000 drachmas for a double in summer, 2,900 drachmas off-season. Next to it is a pension called Christie's, which has similar views. These two, and the Serifos Beach Motel, where we received a churlish reception, were the only ones open in October.

WHERE TO EAT

At Benny's Tavern, on the bay at Livadia, stiff-shouldered, short-haired, choleric Benny, who is Swiss, will play you Mozart's Requiem in the morning and bossa nova in the evening and cook you breakfast himself. Want a little change from taverna fare? Try spring rolls, chicken livers, or whatever suits the fancy of sweet-natured Earl, Benny's skillful, self-taught chef from New York. After two or three days of meals here you will tune into the dramas being played out by the island's German-Swiss-Danish expatriates.

There are several other cafés, juice bars, and fast-food places along the beach and a couple of tavernas in the Chora, open in summer.

Sifnos

This attractive island in the western Cyclades is situated between Serifos, Kimolos, and Anti-Paros. It is 74 square kilometers and has a population of 2,000. Its highest peak is Mt. Profitis Ilias, 680 kilometers.

Your first glimpse of Sifnos is the port town of Kamares. Its freshly whitewashed concrete cubes with colored doors give the town a shipshape, modern feeling. The quayside is lined with tamarisk trees, behind which lie the tavernas and the pottery shops for which the island is famous. (Most of the ceramics are unremarkable, if not downright kitschy.) Unless you are a harbor freak, we suggest you take the bus up to Apollonia, the main town, perhaps allowing a couple of hours to visit Kamares before your departure on the ferry.

It is a brief bus ride (70 drachmas) up from the port to Apollonia. On the way, you will notice that like most of the Cyclades, Sifnos is mountainous. But it is softer, without the sharp ridges of Serifos or the cliffs of Folegandros.

Apollonia and its sister villages, Artemona to the north and Exambela to the south, make a broad band of white buildings looking over a valley and out to sea. A paved road links the three towns, but it is more rewarding to walk the foot/donkey path toward the back of the village. Along the way, note how substantial some of the houses appear; many Sifnians have gone to Athens and made money, we were told. The path eventually leads to the handsome church at Artemona, from which there is an outstanding view of the island, including the Kastro. In mid-October, a rainstorm turned the dry wall terraces green and hung the sky with dark clouds shot with light. An occasional sunbeam singled out a white cottage or blue-domed chapel. The sea moved swiftly southward, dark and silent, and across the channel Paros and Anti-Paros lay placidly in sunlight.

On Sifnos, the medieval walled city is not, for a change, on the mountaintop but on a sheer cliff very near the sea. From Apollonia, you can take the bus or walk (2 km) down to the Kastro. The buses run every half hour or so. (Apollonia has two bus stops. The Kamares bus is in the central square; the Kastro bus on the main road, about 100 yards away.)

The Kastro on Sifnos is, in our opinion, the jewel of Kastros. You climb a little way up the hill and enter the walled city through two or three covered archways. As in the ancient Chora on Folegandros, a row of houses join each other to form an external wall. Facing them is another, internal, row of houses. The houses are freshly white-washed, the trim brightly painted. Grape arbors overhang the streets intermittently, giving shade. There is a great deal of renovation going on, in which you can see classical ruins embedded in the Venetian stonework. In the narrow passageways, two or three Roman sarcophagi are casually parked. In winter, the Kastro has only 80 residents; in summer, when people return home from Athens, there are 400.

Be sure to take the bus out to the stunning white monastery at Chrysopigi, built on a spit jutting out from shore.

We were there on a stormy day, when pewter clouds turned the water inky dark and the sun spotlighted the church dramatically. The wind was blowing so hard it seemed as if it might ring the bells in the bell tower. We watched a fishing boat scurry for shelter into the pretty fishing port of Faros, nearby.

Among the other monasteries on the island are the monastery of Taxiarchis, above the village of Vlathy, and, on top of the mountain of the same name, the monastery of Prophet Elijah, which dates back to the eighth century.

An easy walk farther down the road from Chrysopigi is the beach town of Plati Gialos, which has a handsome long strip of beach and several restaurants and places to stay, including the apparently brand-new Hotel Alexandros, complete with outdoor bar and swimming pool. Off-season, the whole town is completely shut down; you can't even get a cup of coffee.

The history of Sifnos is similar to that of the other Cycladic islands. In ancient times, it was occupied by the Minoans, then the Ionians. It took part in the Persian Wars and joined the Athenian League. It was liberated from a long Turkish domination in the early nineteenth century along with its sister islands.

In ancient times, Sifnos prospered because of its gold and silver mines. Legend has it that because the islands ceased tithing to Apollo, the mines were flooded by the sea, depriving Sifnos of its major source of income and reducing it to poverty. In other versions of this story, the islanders offered the god a gilt egg instead of a solid gold one.

Today, the island has a more prosperous air than its neighbors. It is tightly terraced, with plentiful olive groves and vineyards. Even the donkeys seem sleeker (and the people handsomer?) than elsewhere. The little triangular niches that you see in buildings everywhere are dovecotes. An ample water supply allows for continuing agriculture, and, increasingly, in summer the economy is stimulated by an influx of tourists who appreciate the quiet, the gentle landscape, and the beaches.

HOW TO GET THERE

The ships out of Piraeus which run along the western Cyclades call at Sifnos daily in summer, three or four times a week off-season, weather permitting. Once you are on the island, you will find several travel agencies, each handling business for a different ferryboat line. They will not divulge the other's schedule. The final arbiter on boats is always the port police.

WHERE TO STAY

In Apollonia, the Hotel Anthoussa has spacious, comfortably furnished rooms with private baths and tiny balconies with views. It also has central heating, a rarity in Greece, if you are there in the winter. Its only drawback is that it is right on the main drag through town, noisy with motorcycles. Moderately priced.

Across the street diagonally, the Pension Apollonia has utilitarian rooms with good views and shared bath for 1,500 drachmas off-season. When asked about dependable hot water, the landlady just shrugged.

The Hotel Sifnos, also in Apollonia, was closed when we were there in October.

Just above the monastery at Chrysopigi sits the Hotel Flora, with its pretty red trim and lovely views. In 1989, a room for two at high season went for 3,200 drachmas. It is open from May to early October, depending on the weather. The monastery itself has inexpensive rooms to let in summer. (Tel. 31255 to reserve.)

There are also hotels and rooms to let in Kamares.

WHERE TO EAT

The best taverna we found in Greece is Maggana's, on the square at Artemona, a walk of about one kilometer up from the center of Apollonia. Rather than walk around the long hairpin turn on the road, take the stairs; they are a shortcut. Here you will find grilled meat, various cold salads, and the freshest, most delicate fried calamari we have ever eaten. The friendly cook wears a blue fisherman's cap over his gray curls and is happy to have you come in the kitchen and have a look. It must have been he who gave rise to the reputation of Sifnos chefs as being the best in Greece.

There are other restaurants in the villages on the hillsides, but once you've found this one, you won't want to look further. However, it's not open for lunch. The Hotel Anthoussa has a café that does omelets, pizzas, and the like.

In an attractive location at the top of the road down to the monastery at Chrysopigi is Vassili's, which is reputed to have good food, but it's open only in summer.

In the Kastro, there are two or three simple cafés open in summer; when we were there on a rainy October morning, we had bread and coffee in the tiny general store.

There are agreeable tavernas along the harbor at Kamares; one, O Simos, is up front enough to list goat casserole on the menu. This is a good place to wait for the ferry.

Milos

The western Cyclades contain some of the loveliest spots on earth, and yet they suffer from a strangely unenthusiastic press. Lawrence Durrell called poor Milos "a damnably dull hole of a place." We speculate that first impressions may play a part in this; our own experiences with Milos have been far from boring. We find it quite special.

We first saw Milos from the deck of a ferry as we passed through the western Cyclades one October day. As we entered Milos Bay from the northwest, two white ridgetop villages—Milos town and Tripiti—stood high above us to the east. A row of brightly painted houses along the water later turned out to be the magical fishing village of Klima. Despite guidebooks that called Milos mined out, low-lying, barren, isolated, dry, treeless, and lacking in charm, we decided to go back and investigate.

Our tired, late-night arrival at a mostly windowless and utilitarian hotel felt a bit like checking into a cell block.

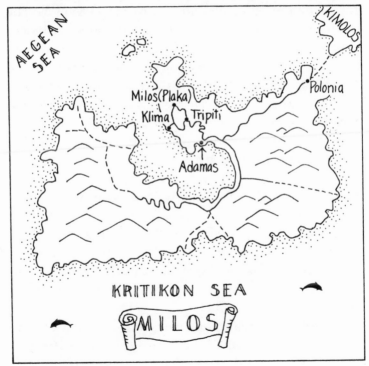

But we had a fine dinner on the waterfront at O Kinigos, where the owner simply came to the table without a menu, slapped down an order pad, and said, "What you want?" Gradually, here as elsewhere, the generosity, the beauty, and the light of Greece began to assert themselves.

In the port town of Adamas, all of the necessities can be found on the harborfront in the block or so south of the ferry dock. These include a comfortable café with the improbable name of Cavo d'Amore, the post office, a bank, ferry ticket offices (which are a good general source of information), car rentals (compare prices), police and customs, and the above-mentioned taverna, O Kinigos. The main bus and taxi terminus is at a square about two blocks south from the ferry.

Before we speak of the history and the substantial commercial life of Milos, let us try to describe some of the beauty of this striking island as we experienced it. Perhaps you will want to explore the same route, but bear in mind that all things change, that three years from now that path off to the left, the one we failed to notice, is the one that leads to magic.

Milos town, locally called *Plaka*, is the modern capital of Milos. It is a lovely Cycladic town—white houses, bright doors and windows—perched on a high ridge overlooking Milos Bay, a few kilometers northwest of Adamas. Buses from Adamas are frequent and cheap; for mobility, we rented an old, tiny, but serviceable car and set out for Milos on a sunny morning.

Milos town and the mountainsides between there, Trapiti, and coastal Klima have been the major settlement areas of Milos since about 1100 B.C. The Dorian Greeks and

their descendants, the Romans, Byzantines, Venetians, Turks, and myriad others passed through. Towering above Milos immediately to the north is a high hill that once held the substantial walled town of the Kastro, the Venetian citadel of Milos for two centuries. Little now stands on the Kastro except churches of relatively recent origin; the Venetian structures have been scavenged for building stone. The church at the very top was destroyed inadvertently by the German army during World War II occupation of Milos and has been rebuilt since that time.

From the Kastro, the highest point on the east side of Milos, there is a panoramic view: white villages, a sparkling patchwork of terraced olive groves, vineyards, white chapels, grain fields just touched with green. Blue sea turns to aquamarine in the protected coves and stretches as far as the eye can see. The eye of the mind looks out on an ancient Greek town, a major Roman city, a Venetian fortress, the Turkish fleet, a German anti-aircraft battery. This spot alone, on a sunwashed day, would justify a trip from Athens.

A short distance south of Milos is the neighboring town of Tripiti, a clifftop site that nearly 2,000 years ago overlooked a large and important Roman town, the original home of the statue Venus de Milo, now in the Louvre. We stopped in search of lunch.

Off the tourist track such things as lunch are always a bit of an adventure. Lunch will be found, and it will be good, but where is it and *what* is it? We found a tiny dingy-looking kafenion with one table on the cliff looking out over one of the places where Christian worship first began. Lunch was salad and bread, which we happily ordered. And ''the little fishes,'' which we declined despite the urging of a friendly hostess. (The "little fishes" were apparently special.) The salad and bread arrived; the bread was delicious. The salads were mostly two heaping plates of tomatoes, bright red chunks, a few olives, and bits of onion and pepper sprinkled with oil. A fine soft cheese came on a side dish. The story of Tripiti is the story of those tomatoes. Linda tasted one of them and almost started to cry. She began talking about moving to Greece—to grow tomatoes. The English language has not yet made room for a tomato like the ambrosia-tomato of Trapiti. And when *you* come to Trapiti, please order "the little fishes." And write to us if they are like its tomatoes.

After lunch, we pointed our tiny car down a narrow lane to the south in search of Klima, the shoreline village we had seen from Milos Bay. We had never driven a car in such streets before. A standard American sedan would not

have fitted the space. One drives s-l-o-w-l-y, watching for children and pets. After a couple of missed turns and an unplanned trip past the Roman catacombs, we wound down a steep hill to Klima. Beware, there are no signs or parking lot; the road simply passes narrowly between two houses and directly into the Aegean.

Klima is a sparkling necklace, a long row of narrow, brightly colored houses strung along a very narrow rock and pebble beach. Most of them are two-story, and the bottom level, only two or three feet above the sea, is a boat house and workshop into which a small fishing boat can be winched. The doors are brilliantly painted; these are what had caught our attention from the ferry and drawn us here. At other fishing ports on Milos, there are sea-level boat houses that are *caves* cut out of the loosely consolidated volcanic ash and debris that forms much of the rock on this

island. The two-story houses of Klima, boat house below, may have evolved from the practice of boat house caves.

We spoke with a fisherman at Klima who as a younger man had worked on ships all over the world. Filled with generosity, he invited us into his cave home and gave us the traditional Greek coffee and glass of water. Then glasses of his own wine. Then he earnestly tried to have us stay for the delicacy of a dinner of grilled octopus. This man had lost a 6-meter fishing boat to a storm a few days earlier, a boat he had built himself. He planned to build another and urged us to come back next year and go fishing with him.

There are other parts of Milos to explore. The island is amply furnished with beaches, especially around the enormous bay, but the best beach is on the south side of the island at Paleohoriou Bay. Here there are many colored stones and two restaurants; nudism is acceptable. A bus goes there every hour from Adamas.

The quiet fishing village of Pollonia is worth a visit. There are no hotels, but there are rooms to let. From Pollonia you can take a day excursion across the narrow strait to the island of Kimolos, where there is one village and some small secluded beaches.

Why are the beauties of Milos such a well-kept secret? The mineral wealth sets the island apart from the rest of the chain. "There's plenty of money here, so we don't advertise," says one resident. "We don't need tourists, but we're happy to have them if they come."

COMMERCIAL MILOS

In fairness to the critics, much of Milos has been ravaged by mining, quarrying, and the shipping of minerals. Some parts of Milos look more like a well-used bombing range than a vacation spot. "Once where there were mountains, there are no mountains," says Nikos, a resident. "Soon the whole island will be flat like an airport." The island is largely volcanic in origin—hot springs and fumeroles tell of continued volcanic activity—and over much of history and prehistory, it has prospered through the export of volcanic minerals as well as agricultural products. In the fifth century B.C., Milos' yearly tax paid to the Athenian League was the same as that paid by the superpowers of the Cyclades, Naxos and Andros, implying considerable wealth. Modern mineral exports include sulfur, alum, perlite, bensonite, barium, kaolin, and pumice as well as a non-volcanic mineral, salt.

Over the long haul of history, Milos' most interesting and important product has been the smooth, easily worked black volcanic glass called obsidian. The edges of obsidian blades are literally as sharp as broken glass. Until quite recently in history, obsidian would have been the knife of choice of any butcher, leather worker, carpenter, or barber. For at least 7,000 years, Milos was essentially the only source of obsidian in the Aegean region and exported it to much of the Mediterranean world. One of the major sources of obsidian on Milos was the low hill just west of Adamas, where chunks can easily be picked up on the surface. (Somewhere we recall reading that in the ancient Aegean world, obsidian was called melitite.)

MILOS IN HISTORY

Milos has been inhabited for at least seven millennia, with settlements scattered over most of the island since about 3500 B.C. There have been two major centers of activity. Between about 3500 B.C. and 1100 B.C., the major ancient city was at Phylacopi, near the northeast end of the island. Excavations show three major periods: Cycladic, Minoan, and Mycenaean. The city at Phylacopi was abandoned in approximately 1100 B.C., at about the time Dorian Greek invaders founded a new settlement north of Milos Bay in the vicinity of modern Milos, Tripiti, and Klima. This part of the island, which includes defensible hilltops with marvelous views, has over the past 3,000 years been the major settlement for successive waves of invaders: the Dorian Greeks, the Romans, Byzantines, Venetians, Turks, and all the lesser armies and pirates that have made Greece such a blood-soaked and relic-strewn part of history. Wherever one walks in the vicinity of Milos town and Tripiti, one sees the ruins, relics, and broken framents of ancient Greek, Roman, and Venetian Milos lying about or built into the walls of modern chapels and homes.

In one incident, the history of Milos differs conspicuously from the rest of the Cyclades. During the Peloponnesian Wars, Milos sided with Sparta against Athens. The result was an Athenian invasion in 416 B.C. in which most of the population of Milos was either destroyed or enslaved. There is a remarkable quotation attributed to Thucydides which summarized this episode as follows: "The Athenians executed all adult Melians they could get their hands on; the women and children they sold into slavery."

HOW TO GET THERE

Olympic Airways runs two-engine, twenty-seat planes from Athens two or three times a week for about $35. The two ferry lines from Piraeus which run the western Cyclades stop here.

WHERE TO STAY

At the extreme north end of the bay at Adamas, set apart from the working harbor, is a small beach with a tight cluster of modern hotels, bland but adequate. No doubt they are busy in summer, but when we were there in mid-October, they were all closed but one, which seemed almost empty and at any rate too dead and far removed to stay in.

There are hotels and rooms to let scattered all over Adamas, but to our taste, the bargain spot is two buildings on the left from the post office, where there are a couple of second-story rooms to let overlooking the harbor for an off-season double rate of 1,600 drachmas.

WHERE TO EAT

In Adamas, the Hotel Adamas has a decent taverna, but our top choice is O Kinigos, on the harborfront. Near the town square and taxi stand, there is a pleasant café that serves yogurt with honey and other light foods. In the village of Zefiria, not far from the airport, try Mama Lula's, where in addition to traditional taverna food and *pitaraki*, the local retsina, they serve up bouzouki music and Greek dancing in the summer.

Anti-Paros

The road to Anti-Paros leads through Paros, one of the most trampled islands in the Cyclades. In prehistoric times, the two islands were joined. In the mid-1960s, the first discovery of a Neolithic site in the Cyclades was made on the adjacent islet of Saliangos, dating human civilization in this complex of islands to 4000 B.C.

Although Paros has its own charm, after the boutiques, rental car offices, and plastic cafés of its capital, Parikia, it is a relief to take the launch across the channel and let your eyes rest on her quieter sister, whose pristine brown hills are very sparsely dotted with white houses, a couple of traditional domed chapels, and a thatched-roof windmill or two.

Every sailor trapped in a storm at sea dreams of a harbor where the water is flat and still, a protected magic cup of a harbor with warm arms encircling a sandy bottom where anchors will hold, a harborfront with a tavern and the hospitality of a human community in waiting. Such a place is the lovely harbor of Anti-Paros. The afternoon light on the water is a jeweled light, a magician's light, a painter's despair. How *could* you render this? Start with something that's halfway between aquamarine and lavender, then stir in a little silver, spit on it, and hope for the best.

Debarking from the launch, we were first and foremost aware that we had arrived at a working port. The annual prewinter boat painting had begun. Steady hands outlined red and blue stripes against the white hulls. Fishermen were unloading boats or mending nets. All was accompanied by the persistent chug of boat engines and the rhythmic slap of fishermen pounding octopus against the stone seawalls.

Along the harbor, there are the usual two or three tav-

ernas, a couple of hotels, and places with rooms to let. Perpendicular to the harbor, a narrow main street lined with shops and cafés slopes gently upward. Winding lanes flanked by whitewashed houses with shutters painted in brilliant colors slither away in both directions like veins from a main artery. As is so often the case, the town is built around the core of a Venetian castle. Although the town is geared for tourists in the summer, most of the invasion consists of day-trippers from Parikia, the harbor at Paros. In late September, half the tourist shops and tavernas were closed, and it felt like the 650 islanders who permanently inhabit the island were repossessing their home. Through open doorways you could see through the tiny, dark houses to sun-washed interior courtyards. Bunches of onions were hanging on walls. Brightly dressed schoolchildren played in the schoolyard. A shopkeeper sat in her doorway tatting lace, a secret smile on her face.

South of the harbor lies a long curve of pebbled beach with clear water but not too much shelter from the wind. On the other side of the harbor, you can walk through a gaggle of geese to another cove with a rather trash-littered sand beach. "No camping or nudding" are allowed here.

At the far end of the island is a deep cave in the mountains about twenty minutes by bus from the village. A lighted concrete staircase descends 100 meters through stalactites and stalagmites. Here, in 1673, a candlelit midnight mass was celebrated on Christmas Eve by archaeologist and French ambassador de Nointel, plus his 500 guests.

The bus, which goes almost to the entrance to the cave, is by far the simplest and most direct way to get there. If you go by boat (many of the day boats from Paros continue on from the village to the caves), you are faced with either a long, hot climb up the mountain or negotiating a donkey ride. Now, if you choose the latter, you may be approached by a gentle muleteer, lively as Zorba, who will fill you with zest for life and remind you why you came to the Cyclades in the first place. We, however, encountered a highway brigand disguised as an innocent old Greek peasant who manipulated us six ways 'til Sunday into overpaying him. Moral: strike a clear bargain and do not let anything but the exact change leave your hands.

Once on the donkey, it is gratifying to be hauled up the hill if you can tolerate the donkey being soundly switched from behind. The donkey driver cries a harsh, gutteral, lip-blowing phrase, the animal clops along steadily, and you are free to gaze at the green-touched hills empty but for a tiny white chapel in the distance. At your back are the sun-kissed water and flat plains dotted with occasional houses.

HOW TO GET THERE

There are flights from Athens to Paros several times a day in summer and daily off-season, plus additional flights from Rhodes and Heraklion (Crete). In high season, small ferries leave from Paros harbor several times a day, and in spring and fall you can count on one or two a day, weather permitting. In winter, the ferry to Parikia no longer makes the crossing, but a boat goes back and forth from the Paros village of Pounta, at the narrowest point on the strait.

WHERE TO STAY

There are small hotels and rooms to let scattered throughout the village. Prices of rooms drop by one-half to two-thirds after the peak months of July and August. For exam-

ple, the nameless place with blue trim opposite the dock charges 2,800 drachmas ($17) for a double room in summer, but the price drops to 1,000 drachmas ($6) off-season. The Mantalena Hotel charges 700 drachmas ($4) per person off-season. The latter has balconies that are particularly fine for photographing the harbor or supervising its activities.

WHERE TO EAT

There are a number of pleasant but undistinguished cafés and tavernas along the harborfront and in the village.

In one of the harborfront tavernas, we had a soft white cheese that was so delicious we asked the proprietor what kind it was. "Anti-Paros cheese," he shot back with satisfaction.

Dodecanese

Folegandros, Serifos, Sifnos, Milos, and Anti-Paros all are located in the Aegean island group known as the Cyclades. Tilos and Kastellorizo, which we will visit next, are in the very different island group called the Dodecanese.

Dodecanese means twelve islands but really describes fourteen islands off the coast of Asia Minor. The term dates back to 1908, when twelve islands organized a protest against Turkey, which had taken away privileges the islands had enjoyed since the days of Süleyman the Magnificent.

One of the dominant forces in the history of these islands is the order of the Knights of St. John—sometimes known as the Knights of Rhodes or the Knights of Malta— which conquered Rhodes in 1306. The architecture of Rhodes and the fortresslike castles on the smaller islands attest to the influence of these Western European warrior knights. After two centuries of domination by the knights, the islands were conquered by the Turks, who controlled them until 1912, then seized by Italy during a war between Italy and Turkey. Italy retained control of them until late in World War II, when Britain occupied them one by one. In

1947, they became a part of the modern Greek state.

To reach Rhodes, the major island in the chain, you can fly from Athens (flights are frequent and cheap), or you can take a *very* long ferry ride from Piraeus. There are also boats and flights from Crete and many ferry connections from other islands in the Aegean.

Although they have a common history, each of these islands, like the Cyclades, has its own character. In addition to the two islands we include here, you might want to visit Symi, with its golden Italianate harbor, or the volcanic island of Nissyros. Both of these are served by the same ferry that goes to Tilos, as well as by day excursion boats from Rhodes. These are just a few of the possibilities in this rich region.

Tilos

Tilos is not in the guidebooks. Lying between Rhodes and Kos in the southern Sporades, this simple, undeveloped island is often confused with the better-known Tinos in the Cyclades. The island is greener than most in this part of the Aegean, covered with olive trees and with a varied agriculture that includes citrus cultivation. Tilians are proud of the fact that their island has its own water; *they* are not dependent on water boats from Rhodes.

There are only two residential towns on Tilos. The harbor at Livadia is a small utilitarian concrete agglomeration on a lovely large bay. Twelve kilometers inland, the livelier, cozier village of Megalo Chorio nestles against the mountainside of Aghios Stefanos, beneath the ruins of the castle of the Knights of St. John, one of seven ruined castles to be found on the island. A third town, Mikro Chorio, has been empty of residents for twenty years.

The harbor town, Livadia, has a long stretch of clean, pebbly beach, and on either side of the town, there are long footpaths along the cliffs which lead eventually to small secluded beaches. There are beaches elsewhere on the island as well, the only sandy one being a couple of kilometers from the inland town of Megalo Chorio, through a valley planted with citrus orchards. In the summer, there is a bus that goes there.

Tilos is a walker's paradise. A beautiful sunrise can be seen from the trails along the cliffs at Livadia. It is also lovely to walk through the fragrant low scrub here in the late afternoon, especially on a day when you can watch a ferry

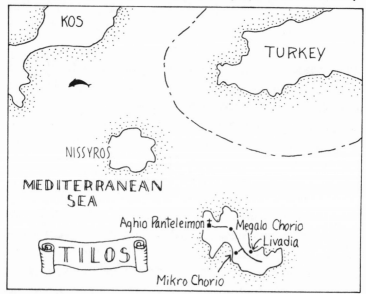

slowly cut its swath into the bay. It is equally satisfying to walk on the inland roads, where at most you will encounter one or two cars and a few scampering goats as you admire the olive trees against the reddish hills and inhale the aroma of sunbaked herbs.

If you are staying in Livadia, you can take a bus to Megalo Chorio and from there hike up to the ruined stone castle of the Knights of St. John, from which you can look down on the green and fertile fields of Tilos and across the water to its small volcanic neighbor, Nissyros. The castle ruins are lumpy stone walls, said to be built on the site of a

temple to Athena. There are still some faint frescoes in the castle's crumbling chapel. To go up the mountain, follow the road around the village which gently disintegrates into a rocky path. Pass the square white water storage building, go through a rickety gate, and keep climbing. The view is worth it, especially if you are lucky enough to be there on a day without haze. This is a half-hour to 45-minute climb, only for the vigorous.

Eight kilometers north of Megalo Chorio is the monastery of Aghio Panteleimon, to which you will have to walk or hitch as there is no bus service. Like most of the monasteries on these small islands, it is deserted, but the building is still maintained. After the hot walk, it is a relief to sit in the pretty courtyard under the huge fig tree and drink from the delicious natural spring.

About halfway between Livadia and Megalo Chorio is a cave in which were found the skeletons of some dwarf elephants. If you tell the bus driver you want to see the caves, he will stop in the middle of nowhere, point you down a path, and tell you to turn left at the olive tree, pass the chapel, and so on. A short but steep climb, with little reward.

The visual jewel of the island is the deserted village of Mikro Chorio, which as late as the 1950s had hundreds of inhabitants. With immigration to Australia and Athens, the village depopulated until the last remaining residents moved to Livadia. Now the buff stones of the roofless square houses blend in with the gently sloping mountainside. All has been left to softly crumble away, all, that is, but the large handsome church that stands—gleaming white and perfectly maintained—under its red-domed roof. This is a sight, when you first come upon it, that is so visually stunning, so surprising in its incongruity, that it stops the heart. Then, as the wind soughs through the yawning archways and empty windows that peer over the terraced valley, the mood of the place comes over you. Stillness. A

silence broken only by a falling stone dislodged by a shaggy wild ram or the cry of a solitary crow. You notice the pomegranate tree that still bears fruit and have thoughts about nature's tenacity and the brevity of our lives.

An old woman speaks about her home: "In Mikro Chorio, it was lovelier than on the coast in Livadia. Next to each house stood an oil press and an oven. We raised sheep and goats and planted our terraces with wheat and barley. We lacked for nothing. But the young people moved away. In the end, no one was left. I was the last to leave the little village in 1967. My house is up there. Now our houses are crumbling. Nobody takes care of them. The fields lie fallow. Only the almonds and olives are harvested."

Mikro Chorio is located about one kilometer up a short road that branches off the main road between Livadia and Megalo Chorio. A sign at the bottom of the road indicates

OTE. The town is about a 45-minute walk from Livadia, or you can ask the bus driver to drop you where the road branches off. Take your camera. Take a notebook. Plan to stay a while.

By the time we reached Tilos, at the end of October, the harbor town was quiet and shuttered. There was only one open restaurant and one set of rooms to let. The weather, after storms earlier in October, was splendid: the air warm and still, the light golden, the water quite swimmable. Hikers, painters, lovers, solitaries, anyone in search of quiet beauty and rest, this is the place.

HOW TO GET THERE

There are ferries, usually the *Papadiamantis* or the *Kimolos*, two or three times a week from Rhodes. Once a week or so, one of the ferries that originates in Piraeus and goes through the Cyclades continues to Amorgos, Astypalea, and the smaller islands of the Dodecanese. To encourage travel to these islands, passage to and from Tilos and its neighbor, Nissyros, is subsidized and free to tourists going to and from Rhodes. If you disembark at Symi, you have to pay.

WHERE TO STAY

The prize for the most pleasant, comfortable place on the island definitely goes to the Hotel Irini, a short distance from the beach in Livadia, which has clean rooms with private baths and views of the ocean and the hills, plus a pretty garden and friendly, English-speaking management. The

price is 4,500 drachmas double; 2,000 off-season. It closes the end of October.

The Hotel Livadia is sloppily run and less than clean, but it is cheap and central. There is a string of houses right along the water with very basic rooms to let. The only one open in late October was the more than reasonable Pension Paradise, very basic, with shared bath and concrete floor, run by a kindly woman who will cook you a tasty, cheap omelet breakfast. If you stay in one of these rooms to let on the bay, off-season, watching the sunset turn the Aegean into pink and blue seersucker as a cormorant glides along diving for fish, you may start to feel like you're in a rest home, it's so peaceful. In Megalo Chorio, there are also rooms and apartments with kitchens available.

WHERE TO EAT

In summer, there are a few eating establishments open along the bay at Livadia. By October, the options narrow down to the traditional, and somewhat forbidding, kafenion on the square, and Kosta's restaurant, just up from the ferry-boat dock. Here townspeople and tourists gather to eat and drink in a big modern room with the television always on in one corner, sound off, and tinny, mournful Greek ballads coming from the radio. The menu is basic Greek international: spaghetti Bolognese, cotelette, calamari, Greek salad, night after night. Fish is expensive and usually frozen. When the tourists are few and stay a few days, both the locals and fellow tourists are friendly. Kosta's mother, a beautiful old woman with fine skin and ruddy cheeks, sits there every night, all in black with a black scarf over her head. People greet her from time to time, but mostly she just looks at the television peacefully, arms folded across her chest. The taverna is her living room.

There is also a small taverna and a traditional kafenion in Megalo Chorio.

Kastellorizo (Meghisti)

"After we found Kastellorizo, all other Greek islands died for us."
—Uwe Redlich, Hamburg

Tiny Kastellorizo, three miles off the coast of Turkey, has been described as a corner of Europe. Because of its strategic location between Rhodes and Cyprus and its natural protected harbor, it has been occupied by many nations. It

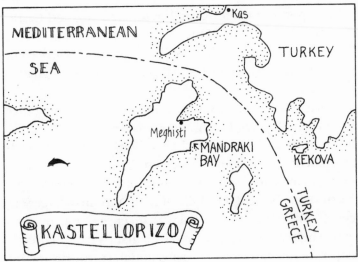

was first settled by Crete, then Dorian Greeks from Rhodes in the eleventh century, followed by Persians, Arabs, Saracens, the Knights of St. John, Neapolitans, Turks, and Venetians. For a time in the eighteenth century, it even served as a Russian naval base, and in the early part of this century, it belonged to Italy. It did not become a part of Greece until 1947, along with the rest of the Dodecanese.

The island prospered as a trading center until early in this century, when it failed to make the changeover from sailboats to steamboats. With economic decline, there was a massive emigration to Australia, where there are now said to be upward of 20,000 Kastellorizans. Used as a fuel and munitions depot during World War II, the island was evacuated before it was heavily bombed by the Germans. Many of the islanders did not return after the war, so the island's population has now been reduced to about 250 residents.

Its popular name, Kastellorizo, meaning Red Castle, comes from the name of the castle the knights built on the island, the ruins of which can still be seen. The original name of the island was Meghisti, and this is its official designation today.

Kastellorizo has a softer, more protected feeling than most of the Aegean. Facing Turkey, its beautiful natural harbor is lined with two-story houses with peaked tile roofs and balconies painted blue, brown, or green. Some of the houses are white, some pale gold or blue, some simply worn stone. Behind the circle of houses looms a larger circle of stony mountains dotted with green, as if the toy town were sheltered and shadowed by a giant's hand. Directly opposite the harbor lie the substantial, storm-protecting

mountains of the Turkish coast, furthering the sensation of being in a cozy, protected cup.

The east end of the harbor is marked by the minaret of an unused mosque, a mark of the island's deep historical ties with its continental neighbor. Above and behind it is the small, thoughtful museum with its display of relics found on the island (open mornings, admission free). Over them both tower the ruins of a medieval castle, from which an enormous Greek flag waves defiantly at the Turkish mainland. Toward the middle of the harbor under three white archways is the old fish market, with its stone tables.

In summer, the harbor here is packed with sailboats, mostly rented by European vacationers cruising the Turkish coast. The waiters and shopkeepers watch the boaters come in—first the Germans and English in spring, then the Italians in high season, then the Germans again during their

Oktoberfest, when the children are out of school. "They change with the seasons," says one of the owners of a harborfront taverna, "like fruit." When we arrived in October, there were still fifteen boats in the harbor, but they were all gone a few days later.

Kastellorizo's colorful rectangular harbor is a photographer's dream. For one of the best views, take the steep path up the mountain behind the village. There is a monastery at the top.

Swimming is good on the island. There are no beaches as such, but the water off the rocks is warm and clear. Even if you are not staying there, the people at the Hotel Meghisti don't seem to mind if you swim off their terrace. Or walk behind the hotel and over to the next cove, below the chapel of Aghio Stefano, where there is a good spot to swim. If you walk up the hill past the O Platania restaurant and the cemetery, you can find some body-sized patches of sand among the rocks at the edge of the water.

You can hire a motorized raft and driver to take you for a bouncy and inelegant 20-minute ride to the Blue Grotto, where you must duck down in the raft to enter the huge, vaulted cave, which measures 150 x 80 meters and has a 35-meter ceiling. Here you can swim in the gentle, light-infused waves. If you have never been in a grotto before, this is definitely worth doing. It was not until we got home that we read Lawrence Durrell's comments about this excursion: "The grottoes are finer than those of Capri, but the visit has to be carefully calculated; for, when the sea rises under wind, the entrances get blocked, and there is a risk of being trapped inside." Still, we agree with Durrell, who concludes, "It is worth the risk and effort. Go!"

Another pretty spot is Mandraki Bay, just east of the harbor. This was once the wealthy part of town, where the shipowners had their homes. Now most are crumbling ruins, devastated by earthquakes or World War II bombs. There is almost no reconstruction. Since many people evacuated the island during the war and did not return, the status of the houses is in limbo and they cannot be restored.

If you go around the harbor to your right, past the stairway to the museum and the minaret, follow the coastal path, and climb the steep, uneven stairs upward, you will come to a splendid tomb, a shelved stone cavern that looks out over the water. The stone portico, which has many counterparts along the Turkish coast dating from the Lycian culture in Asia Minor, is a stunning blend of terra-cotta, cream, and gray stone. This is a good place to sit for an hour watching the boats pull into the harbor and con-

templating the nearby Turkish coast. By late afternoon the mountains and town are in shadow, but a rose-gold light laps at the tiny white stone island just outside the entrance to the harbor.

It is impossible to talk about Kastellorizo without talking about Turkey. For one thing, most of the food in the restaurants is grown in the Turkish valleys just beyond the coast range; boats from the island make the shopping trip two or three times a week, which is much easier and cheaper than going all the way to Rhodes. In turn, Turkish excursion boats bring day visitors to the island; the boatmen sit around and play backgammon with the Greek waiters while their passengers wander the island.

For about 2,000 drachmas ($12.50) per person, we arranged a day excursion from Kastellorizo to Kas, a Turkish coastal town just across from the island, on one of the fishing boats. Ask an English-speaking restaurant employee which boat might next be making the trip. When you arrive in Kas, your passport will be held by an official for the day, so be sure and take cash other than Greek currency to change for Turkish lire. The banks do not want Greek money and will not cash traveler's checks without a passport.

The boat trip to Kas takes about half an hour. From offshore, you can see minarets and a beautiful old Greek amphitheater. Kas is an attractive, rather touristy town with a busy marina. There is a pleasant small market just behind the harborfront. (Cooks take note: saffron is cheap here!)

From Kas, we took a lengthy excursion by boat (10,000 Turkish lire, or $7) down the coast to Kekova, a small island with the remains of an ancient city on it. To visit this, you must do some tricky clambering over the rocks from the boat tied up offshore. If you do not wish to disembark, you can at least view the ruin of a Byzantine church from the boat. Quick stops are made at two coastal villages, one for lunch (terrific food!) and the other to view more ruins.

Both villages feel poor and isolated; the influx of tourists on boats must be fairly recent. Pretty little village girls, heads covered, hang around the restaurants with baskets of colorful scarves for sale. The boat also passes by a submerged city, but you can't see much. If you have never been to Turkey, this gives you a quick bite of its rural life and a sense of the ancient civilizations that have succeeded one another here.

Pulling out of the harbor at Kas, we could hear the (taped) Muslim call to prayer from the minarets. From the mast of our boat, tiny Turkish and Greek flags flew side by side under the stars. As we drew closer to the island, the lights of Kas receded, and from the Kastellorizo kafenion came the familiar sound of Greek bouzouki music blasting over the radio. We had bridged two cultures in a day.

A few northern Europeans have been coming to Kastellorizo for years; they have learned Greek and have formed close connections with the islanders. Now that they have discovered this remote, beautiful, special place, they want to pull up the drawbridge behind them. And who can blame them? But a moderate number of tourists infuse money into the local economy and generate an exchange of energy from the outside world. In fact, without tourists, Kastellorizo would shrivel up and turn in on itself altogether. Even now, the population is down to around 250, and those receive a small government subsidy to remain on the island. Go pay them a visit. Take the trouble to seek out this lovely spot.

HOW TO GET THERE

Kastellorizo has a tiny airport consisting of a one-room building and a slit in the hills for a runway. The twice-weekly flights to Rhodes in Olympic's sturdy little two-engine, twenty-seat planes leave at 9:00 a.m. and take about 45 minutes. The cost is 4,420 drachmas ($27) one way. The bus from the airport to the village costs 200 drachmas ($1.20).

Passage to and from Rhodes by boat is free, to encourage tourism, and takes about six hours. The *Papadiamantis* leaves between 6:00 and 8:00 p.m. and gets to Rhodes at the inconvenient hour of 3:00 a.m. However, tourists are sometimes allowed to sleep on the boat until dawn. A faster boat leaves during the day once a week.

WHERE TO STAY

Hotel Meghisti, at the far left end of the harbor, has a large terrace with a beautiful view, and you can step off the edge for a swim. Because it's the only hotel, they can get away with charging rather high prices for a remote island, 4,000 drachmas for a double.

There are several places with rooms to let. We stayed at Christalo's, a few steps away from the harbor, which was very pleasant and quiet. It has three upstairs rooms with peaceful views of the hills and a shared terrace and bath. Ask someone in one of the restaurants for directions. The tiny pale blue pension with the good view two doors from the hotel is reputed to have terrible beds. Pension Barbara has no view, no terrace, and no hot water, but it's cheap.

WHERE TO EAT

"Why do you want to go to Kastellorizo?" the Olympic Airways clerk asked us. "There won't be any restaurants or hotels. You may have trouble getting something to eat."

We found more eating choices here than on any other small Greek island. There are four restaurants, a bar, and a kafenion along the harborfront, plus one set back a little from it on the main square and another behind the old central market with the archways. In addition, there is O Platania, high up the steps behind the village, which is our favorite. You may have to ask directions to O Platania. In the back of the village, there are some steps that lead up to a large square where the school and two churches are located. To the right, there is a small building with a few tables outside.

The taverna, which takes its name from the nearby plane tree, is run by two women, Maria and Evangelia, who are the essence of Greek warmth and hospitality. Here you won't find fish, or spaghetti Bolognese, or cotelette, only one or two simply cooked meat dishes and enormous Greek salads. They also make a delicious, well-seasoned croquette with garbanzo bean flour. Called *revithopites*, it is a Greek version of falafel. If you ask for a sweet, out comes homemade preserved fig and orange rind, *very* sweet. A slow meal under the stars up here on a warm evening, laughter coming from the kitchen and the little red light glowing on the church across the way, is the essence of simple pleasure.

Orea Meghisti is a bit back from the harbor, under a grape arbor. It is run by a family of reverse immigrants from Australia who came back to stay a few years ago. All are fluent in English and happy to talk about the island. The food is good, too, especially the grilled meat. They raise some of it themselves on a nearby small island.

Two restaurants stand side by side front and center of the harbor. When the yachts come in, the men compete to help the sailors tie up. Our favorite is Lazarikis. The food is not out of the ordinary, but how can you resist a Greek that looks like Dudley Moore? George and his brother Lazarus, both charming, speak English and bring in customers for their parents' cooking.

Little Paris (God only knows why the name) is a grubby place, just down the harborfront from Lazarikis. It serves the best fresh fish in town and lovely fresh feta as well.

TURKEY

It was almost impossible to obtain any advance information about Turkish islands. Guidebooks never mentioned them, and even a letter from the Turkish Embassy was discouraging. Many reliable sources wrote that inhabited Mediterranean islands did not exist. We were ready to omit Turkey completely when a friend came to the rescue with the *Yachting Guide to Turkey.* Here were photos, the first solid proof that two inhabited islands *did* exist! Alibey Adasi ("Adasi" is the Turkish for "island") seemed relatively easy to reach without a private yacht, but the logistics of how to get to Bozcaada Adasi would have to wait until we reached Turkey. Even with actual names, no one could supply any information about how to get there. Taking two precious paragraphs from the *Yachting Guide,* we left for Turkey. Happily, both islands proved to be well worth the effort.

Spanning two continents, with a 10,000-year-old cultural heritage, Turkey is one of the world's most exotic destinations. Like ancient Rome and Greece, the Ottoman Empire was an early world power extending from Africa through the Middle East and into Central Europe. You can find important remnants of that empire throughout the Aegean and Mediterranean; ancient ruins line the 4,890 miles of coastline. Within a few hours of Bozcaada and Alibey islands is Homer's Troy, site of the epic struggle depicted in the *Iliad*. Also nearby is Alexandria Troas, a prosperous and powerful city-state in both Hellenistic and Roman times. To the south is Pergamon, the cultural center that was home to one of antiquity's great libraries, which housed more than 200,000 books. The theater (seating 15,000), the altar of Zeus, the temples, and the agora are situated on a dramatic site atop a steep hill. And near Pergamon's Acropolis are the ruins of the Asklepion, one of the most important medical centers in ancient times. Ephesus, farther south, the leading port in the second century A.D., was the commercial and population center of the western Mediterranean. Built in the imperial manner, the city has monumental temples, baths, public ways, and a theater that continues to host cultural events to this day. Within its boundaries was one of the Seven Wonders of the World, the Temple of Artemis.

Since medieval times, Christians have marked a visit to Ephesus among the holiest of pilgrimages. Today you can also see the little chapel at the site where the Virgin Mary spent her final days. Among those who rode in processionals on Ephesus' Arcadian Way were Mark Antony and Cleopatra. Here, too, St. Paul preached in the theater (there was seating for 25,000) against the Ephesians' goddess Artemis. A cool reception to his criticism, particularly from local merchants, persuaded him to leave town. Afterward, he sent epistles to the Ephesians.

Turkish cuisine is one of the finest in the world. We know American chefs who vacation in Turkey for the food alone. What makes eating special is the freshness, variety, and blend of flavors and the high-intensive labor that goes into its preparation. Try the *patlican salatasi* (puréed eggplant mixed with yogurt); *coban salatasi* (chopped tomatoes, cucumbers, parsley, olives, and spicy peppers); *borek* (pastry rolls filled with white cheese and parsley, then deep fried); and dozens of fancy kebabs. The cafés do not expect you to be an expert on Turkish cuisine; they have a sample order of most dishes on display behind glass counters. On our first trip, we just pointed and tried as many items as we could. You can afford to experiment, as prices are reasonable.

Alibey Adasi

A horse-drawn farmer's wagon on Alibey Adasi was our first glimpse of Turkey from the deck of the Greek ferry bound for Ayvalik on the Turkish mainland. Alibey Town appeared next, with dozens of colorful fishing boats crowding the waterfront. The local mosque assured us that we had left Europe behind. The ferry passed Alibey to dock on the mainland a few miles away.

On land, the color and excitement of Turkey are immediately apparent. A happy bazaar atmosphere overwhelms the senses: the sound of horse-drawn carts on narrow streets; the aroma of herbs, spices, and coffee; the visual treat of so many interesting-looking people and enticing shops.

A bridge connects Alibey with the mainland, so now there is the choice of arriving by ferry or by taxi. Neither the water nor the land approach bypasses the ugly concrete housing projects that cover a barren hillside. The charm of Çunda (pronounced ''JUN-da''), known also as Alibey Town, is a welcome contrast. Once a prosperous Greek town (the island became part of Turkey with the Treaty of Lausanne in 1923), there are many fine examples of neoclassical architecture, picturesque half-ruined houses, an abandoned Greek church, a lively waterfront promenade, and several small hotels that welcome the tired traveler with a comfortable bed and food to please the most particular gourmand.

Even in late September, the midday heat and intense light discourage exploration; dawn is the perfect time to watch the island come to life. First to appear are the farmers who bring their produce to stores that have pastel-tinted walls faded by decades of sunlight. A black goat grazes

against the remains of a mottled green wall that glistens from the rays of the early morning sun. Old women appear from behind ornately carved doors to wash their steps with buckets of water, a tradition performed for centuries. Next, the cat population begins to stir, then to amble down toward the waterfront for the arrival of the fishermen with the daily catch. Birds flutter through the empty windows of a now-abandoned Greek church. Inside are water-damaged frescoes and exposed brick columns that are hauntingly beautiful. Around 8:00 a.m., small, happy groups of children walk down the quiet streets to their elementary school behind the yacht harbor. Their black jackets, shorts, and newly pressed white shirts are spotless. Some of the youngsters have put an elegant finishing touch to their uniform, a starched white handkerchief in the tiny jacket pocket. The waterfront cafés fill up for morning tea,

and then with the arrival of the fishing boats, the cats are fed and the midday meal is delivered in handmade baskets to the restaurants and hotels. The day is in full swing in Çunda; life moves with gusto and much pleasure on this now shimmering Turkish island.

Swimming is disappointing near the town, but the northern part of the island is a magnificent forest of aromatic pine trees that cascade down to quiet coves of enticing blue-green water. Back in Çunda, a variety of food that is almost mind-boggling for a small island awaits the famished swimmer.

In the evening, young and old enjoy a leisurely stroll up and down the waterfront. More active nightlife is available only 15 minutes away in Ayvalik.

HOW TO GET THERE

Flights from Athens, Greece, to Lesbos take only 35 minutes and cost $38. During the summer, there is regular

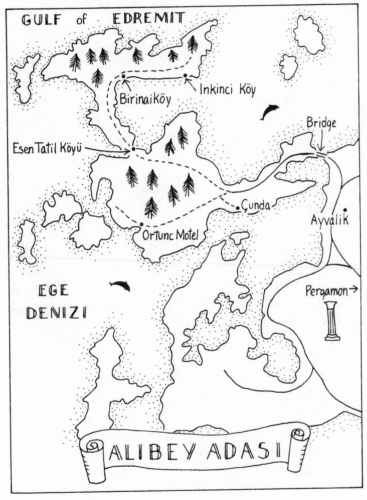

ferry service from Lesbos to Ayvalik for $20. The Monday, Wednesday, Friday service may soon be expanded, as there are now two excellent Greek boats that leave at 9:00 a.m. from the harbor terminal near the Blue Sea Hotel and return at 5:00 p.m. Reserve and purchase tickets at any of the several agencies along the waterfront. The smaller Turkish ferry looked inviting and is probably less expensive. Crossing time is approximately two hours. Off-season, boats operate once a week unless winter storms halt service completely. The boat docks in Ayvalik, Turkey, one block from the main street where taxis are available for approximately $4 for the ride to Çunda town (7 km). The bus fare is 20¢, and there are frequent water taxis and small ferries during the summer months.

WHERE TO STAY

Artur Restoran ve Motel (Alibey Adasi, Ayvalik, Turkey; tel. 663-71014) has eight clean, comfortable rooms with private baths above an appealing waterfront restaurant. Rooms on the front face the promenade and bay, while the rooms in back have a bird's-eye view of life along a narrow street where locals gather to gossip, play games, and eat. Room rates here are very inexpensive.

Gunay Restoran and Motel (Gomeclinin Yeri, Alibey Adasi, Ayvalik, Turkey; tel. 663-71048) is one block from the waterfront behind a park with swings for children; this charming restaurant has several rooms upstairs with private bath. Very inexpensive (under $15 for two).

Ortunc Motel (Alibey Adasi, Ayvalik, Turkey; tel. 663-71120) is located in the pine forest a few miles from town.

Each of the very moderately priced rooms has a private outdoor terrace facing an idyllic cove. Hiking trails abound. An outdoor restaurant faces the beach.

WHERE TO EAT

It is probably impossible to get a bad meal anywhere on Alibey Adasi. There are many pleasant open-air waterfront restaurants with indoor seating for the off-season. The local favorite is Gomeçli.

Bozcaada Adasi

Bozcaada is the ancient Tenedos, home of Apollo Smintheus, god of mice, and the base for the Greek attack on Troy. In Byzantine times, during the reign of Justinian, huge granaries were built so that ships carrying grain to Constantinople could be unloaded here and the grain ferried up the Dardanelles by small freighters. Nothing remains of the granaries, but the Genovese castle built to protect the harbor is still an impressive sight as the ferry arrives from the mainland. The long journey to get here is rewarded with many undiscovered charms: quiet beaches, fascinating architecture, numerous excellent restaurants, and a waterfront town that is travel-poster perfect but remains totally devoid of tourists. Late afternoon is an ideal time to explore Bozcaada. The island has only twelve miles of paved road so there is no need to rush. Rarely does another vehicle appear, and when one does, it is usually an army truck bound for its unobtrusive military base behind the town.

Stop at the small marble fountain of the now-abandoned church of St. Friday and peer through cracks in the boarded windows of the tiny church. Just down the hill is Ayasma Beach, a long stretch of clean white sand that invites a reflective stroll. It is easy to imagine ancient ships on the horizon making their way to Ephesus or Alexandria Troas. If you are here during the summer, a small café provides drinks and simple meals for the visiting Turks from the mainland and the very occasional intrepid world traveler.

Completing the circle and heading back toward town, the road curves gently through an idyllic valley. Old houses, some with columns of ancient cedar trees, dot the landscape. Beyond, the sea is an aqua-tinted mirage looming behind acres of verdant farmland.

Descending into the town again, the harbor hums with activity. Below the castle, the café is always busy. Many of the chatting customers drinking tea and admiring the view are unaccompanied Turkish women, their heads covered according to custom. Unusual for Moslem Turkey, these small groups of middle-aged women go out and definitely enjoy the ritual of evening tea with friends. Afterward, they will stroll to the far end of the marina to catch the last of the twilight behind the castle.

"My grandfather was born here and I visited him every summer," Dimitris Gelou told us. He is a Greek composer

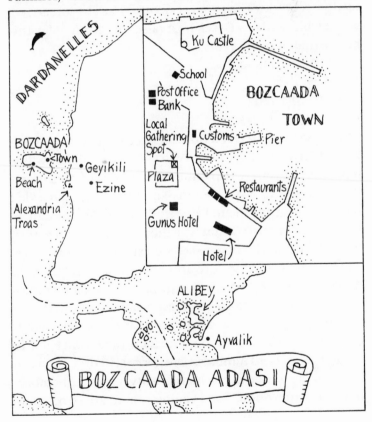

we met on the ferry. "The island was still Greek then. But today only 77 Greeks remain out of 2,700 inhabitants. The island is even quieter now than in the past; you can't say that about many places today. This is truly an island in time; I only wish I could visit more often."

Dinner at Liman Lokantesi is delicious. The meal starts with *meze*, all sorts of appetizers (borek, olives, dolmas, cacik, and coban salatasi), and proceeds to calamari, followed by two whole, fresh Lufer (bluefish) grilled to perfection. A bottle of Talau, the celebrated local wine, arrives at the table, and our Greek host raises his glass: "May this be the first of many visits."

"We'll drink to that!"

HOW TO GET THERE

The easiest way to reach Bozcaada is to rent a car in Ayvalik and drive north to the ferry in Oduniskelesi. Allow five hours for a leisurely trip, time for the ruins of Alexandria Troas along the way. There is an excellent, uncrowded highway from Ayvalik to Ezine (follow the signs to Canakkale, a large industrial town farther north). In Ezine, turn left to Geyikili. (If you pass a Mobil station on your right, you have gone too far. Turn around and take the first road to your right.) The intersection in exotic Geyikili is confusing. Take the second right, an especially wide curve that becomes a narrow one-lane road that twists and winds down to the sea. (Approximate driving time from Ezine to Oduniskelesi is 40 minutes.) The ferry schedule is posted in the ticket window; the boat usually leaves early morning, early afternoon, and evening. There are two restaurants and a superb uncrowded beach to pass the time before the ferry departure. The passenger fare is 30¢ each way (a bargain considering the journey takes 1½ hours). Your car will be useful on the island, or you can leave it in the "parking lot" (no charge). For those with much more time, it is possible to take a bus to Ezine, then a public taxi van to the ferry. Another alternative is to take the direct bus to Canakkale and to sail from there to Bozcaada. (Ferry service is less frequent from Canakkale.)

WHERE TO STAY

Bozcaada is not geared for foreign tourists, and accommodations are very basic. There are four small hotels and pensions that cater to Turkish tourists as well as the very rare foreigner. Hotels are relatively empty except in scorching July and August, when it would be a good idea to have the tourist bureau in Ayvalik call ahead to reserve a room.

Gunus Oteli (Bozcaada Adasi, Turkey; tel. 1252) has wonderful views from the front corner rooms. This modest hotel faces the center town plaza and waterfront restaurants. Shower and toilet are shared down the hall. The back rooms face the town mosque, which reminds you four times a day (and night) that you are in a Moslem country. A room is moderately priced but not the bargain found elsewhere in Turkey.

The modern, charmless Zafer Motel (Bozcaada Adasi, Turkey; tel. 1078) is a five-minute walk above the town and has a superb view of the harbor and castle. The hotel closes in late September for the winter season.

Other lodgings include the Koz Hotel (tel. 1189) and the Emir o'qlu Pansiyon (tel. 1037).

WHERE TO EAT

For what Bozcaada lacks in comfortable lodging, it more than compensates with many excellent, inexpensive restaurants. You cannot go wrong at any of the waterfront cafés: Liman Lokantasi, Koz, Bozcaada Shai, or the beachfront Bozcaada Ayamza on Ayamza Beach.

vinC '89

Other Books from John Muir Publications

Asia Through the Back Door, 3rd ed., Rick Steves and John Gottberg (65-48-3) 336 pp. $15.95

Being a Father: Family, Work, and Self, Mothering Magazine (65-69-6) 176 pp. $12.95

Buddhist America: Centers, Retreats, Practices, Don Morreale (28-94-X) 400 pp. $12.95

Bus Touring: Charter Vacations, U.S.A., Stuart Warren with Douglas Bloch (28-95-8) 168 pp. $9.95

Catholic America: Self-Renewal Centers and Retreats, Patricia Christian-Meyer (65-20-3) 325 pp. $13.95

Complete Guide to Bed & Breakfasts, Inns & Guesthouses, 1990-91 ed., Pamela Lanier (65-43-2) 504 pp. $15.95

Costa Rica: A Natural Destination, Ree Strange Sheck (65-51-3) 280 pp. $15.95

Elderhostels: The Students' Choice, Mildred Hyman (65-28-9) 224 pp. $12.95

Europe 101: History & Art for the Traveler, Rick Steves and Gene Openshaw (28-78-8) 372 pp. $12.95

Europe Through the Back Door, 9th ed., Rick Steves (65-42-4) 432 pp. $16.95

Floating Vacations: River, Lake, and Ocean Adventures, Michael White (65-32-7) 256 pp. $17.95

Gypsying After 40: A Guide to Adventure and Self-Discovery, Bob Harris (28-71-0) 264 pp. $12.95

The Heart of Jerusalem, Arlynn Nellhaus (28-79-6) 312 pp. $12.95

Indian America: A Traveler's Companion, Eagle/Walking Turtle (65-29-7) 424 pp. $16.95

Mona Winks: Self-Guided Tours of Europe's Top Museums, Rick Steves and Gene Openshaw (28-85-0) 450 pp. $14.95

The On and Off the Road Cookbook, Carl Franz (28-27-3) 272 pp. $8.50

The People's Guide to Mexico, Carl Franz (28-99-0) 608 pp. $15.95

The People's Guide to RV Camping in Mexico, Carl Franz with Steve Rogers (28-91-5) 256 pp. $13.95

Preconception: A Woman's Guide to Preparing for Pregnancy and Parenthood, Brenda Aikey-Keller (65-44-0) 236 pp. $14.95

Ranch Vacations: The Complete Guide to Guest and Resort, Fly-Fishing, and Cross-Country Skiing Ranches, Eugene Kilgore (65-30-0) 392 pp. $18.95

Schooling at Home: Parents, Kids, and Learning, Mothering Magazine (65-52-1) $14.95

The Shopper's Guide to Mexico, Steve Rogers and Tina Rosa (28-90-7) 224 pp. $9.95

Ski Tech's Guide to Equipment, Skiwear, and Accessories, edited by Bill Tanler (65-45-9) 144 pp. $11.95

Ski Tech's Guide to Maintenance and Repair, edited by Bill Tanler (65-46-7) 144 pp. $11.95

A Traveler's Guide to Asian Culture, Kevin Chambers (65-14-9) 224 pp. $13.95

Traveler's Guide to Healing Centers and Retreats in North America, Martine Rudee and Jonathan Blease (65-15-7) 240 pp. $11.95

Undiscovered Islands of the Caribbean, Burl Willes (28-80-X) 216 pp. $12.95

Undiscovered Islands of the Mediterranean, Linda Lancione Moyer and Burl Willes (65-53-X) 224 pp. $14.95

22 Days Series

These pocket-size itineraries are a refreshing departure from ordinary guidebooks. Each author has an in-depth knowledge of the region covered and offers 22 tested daily itineraries through their favorite destinations. Included are not only "must see" attractions but also little-known villages and hidden "jewels" as well as valuable general information.

22 Days Around the World by R. Rapoport and B. Willes (65-31-9)
22 Days in Alaska by Pamela Lanier (28-68-0)
22 Days in the American Southwest by R. Harris (28-88-5)
22 Days in Asia by R. Rapoport and B. Willes (65-17-3)
22 Days in Australia, 3rd ed., by John Gottberg (65-40-8)
22 Days in California by Roger Rapoport (28-93-1)
22 Days in China by Gaylon Duke and Zenia Victor (28-72-9)

22 Days in Europe, 5th ed., by Rick Steves (65-63-7)
22 Days in Florida by Richard Harris (65-27-0)
22 Days in France by Rick Steves (65-07-6)
22 Days in Germany, Austria & Switzerland, 3rd ed., by Rick Steves (65-39-4)
22 Days in Great Britain, 3rd ed., by Rick Steves (65-38-6)
22 Days in Hawaii, 2nd ed., by Arnold Schuchter (65-50-5)
22 Days in India by Anurag Mathur (28-87-7)
22 Days in Japan by David Old (28-73-7)
22 Days in Mexico, 2nd ed., by S. Rogers and T. Rosa (65-41-6)
22 Days in New England by Anne Wright (28-96-6)
22 Days in New Zealand by Arnold Schuchter (28-86-9)
22 Days in Norway, Denmark & Sweden by R. Steves (28-83-4)
22 Days in the Pacific Northwest by R. Harris (28-97-4)
22 Days in Spain & Portugal, 3rd ed., by Rick Steves (65-06-8)
22 Days in the West Indies by C. & S. Morreale (28-74-5)

All 22 Days titles are 128 to 152 pages and $7.95 each, except *22 Days Around the World* and *22 Days in Europe*, which are 192 pages and $9.95.

"Kidding Around"
Travel Guides for Children

Written for kids eight years of age and older. Generously illustrated in two colors with imaginative characters and images. An adventure to read and a treasure to keep.